CROCHET

Beautiful Baby Boutique™

Designs by Rebecca Leigh

General Information

Many of the products used in this pattern book can be purchased from local craft, fabric and variety stores, or from the Annie's Attic Needlecraft Catalog *(see Customer Service information on page 31)*.

Contents

Tulip Time

SKILL LEVEL

INTERMEDIATE

FINISHED SIZES

Fits 17-inch chest *(6 months)* [18-inch chest *(12 months)*]
Pattern is written for smaller size with changes for larger size in brackets. When only 1 number is given, it applies to both sizes.

FINISHED MEASUREMENT

Chest: 18 [19] inches

MATERIALS

❏ Bernat Softee Baby fine (sport) weight yarn (5 oz/455 yds/ 140g per skein):
2 skeins MC, 1 skein CC
❏ Sizes B/1/2.25mm [D/3/ 3.25mm] and C/2/2.75mm [E/4/3.5mm] crochet hooks or sizes needed to obtain gauge
❏ Sewing needle
❏ 2 yds 1-inch-wide sheer ribbon
❏ Floral lace appliqué
❏ 3 paper ½-inch roses
❏ Hook-and-loop fastener
❏ White sewing thread
❏ Stitch markers

GAUGE

Size B hook: 10 hdc = 2 inches
Size D hook: 9 hdc = 2 inches

SPECIAL STITCHES

V-stitch (V-st): (Dc, ch 2, dc) in indicated st or sp.
Beginning V-stitch (beg V-st): (Ch 5, dc) in indicated st or sp.
Back post single crochet (bpsc): Insert hook from back to front to back around **post** *(see Stitch Guide)* of indicated st, yo, draw up a lp, complete sc.

INSTRUCTIONS

DRESS
Yoke

Row 1: Beg at neck with size B [D] hook, ch 59 with MC, sc in 2nd ch from hook, sc in each rem ch across, turn. *(58 sc)*

Row 2: Ch 1, sc in each of first 9 sc, 3 sc in next sc *(corner made)*, sc in each of next 9 sc, 3 sc in next sc *(corner made)*, sc in each of next 18 sc, [3 sc in next sc *(corner made)*, sc in each of next 9 sc] twice, turn. *(66 sc)*

Row 3: Ch 2 *(counts as first hdc throughout)*, hdc in each sc across, working 3 hdc in center sc of each 3-sc corner group, turn. *(74 hdc)*

Rows 4–10: Rep row 3. *(130 hdc at end of row 10)*

Row 11: Ch 2, hdc in each of next 18 sts, *ch 8 for armhole, sk next 27 sts*, hdc in each of next 38 sts, rep from * to *, hdc in each of last 19 sts, turn. *(76 hdc)*

Rnd 12: Now working in rnds, ch 2, hdc in same st as joining, hdc in each rem hdc and in each ch around, join with sl st in 2nd ch of beg ch-2. Do not fasten off. Turn. *(93 hdc)*

Skirt

Rnd 1 (RS): With size C [E] hook and MC, ch 4 *(counts as first tr throughout)*, tr in next hdc, ch 1, [sk next hdc, tr in each of next 2 hdc, ch 1] around, join with sl st in 3rd ch of beg ch-4. *(31 ch-1 sps)*

Rnd 2: Ch 1, sc in same st as joining, ch 4, sk 2 sts, sc in next st, ch 4, [sk next st, sc in next st, ch 4] around, ending with sk last st, join with sl st in beg sc. *(46 ch-4 sps)*

Rnd 3: Sl st in first sp, ch 3 *(counts as first dc throughout)*, 6 dc in same sp, *ch 1, dc in next sp, ch 1**, 7 dc in next sp, rep from * around, ending last rep at **, join with sl st in 3rd ch of beg ch-3.

Rnd 4: Sl st in next dc, (sl st, ch 3) in next dc, dc in each of next 2 dc, *ch 1, sk ch-1 sp, **V-st** *(see Special Stitches)* in next dc, ch 1**, dc in each of 3 center dc of next 7-dc group, rep from * around, ending last rep at **, join with sl st in 3rd ch of beg ch-3.

Rnd 5: Sl st in next dc, ch 4 *(counts as first dc, ch-1)*, *7 dc in next V-st sp, ch 1**, dc in center dc of next 3-dc group, ch 1, rep from * around, ending last rep at **, join with sl st

in 3rd ch of beg ch-4.

Rnd 6: Beg V-st *(see Special Stitches)* in same st as joining, *ch 1, dc in each of 3 center dc of next 7-dc group, ch 1**, sk next ch-1 sp, V-st in next dc, rep from * around, ending last rep at **, join with sl st in 3rd ch of beg ch-5.

Rnd 7: Sl st in V-st sp, ch 3, 6 dc in same sp, *ch 1, dc in center dc of next 3-dc group, ch 1**, 7 dc in next V-st sp, rep from * around, ending last rep at **, join with sl st in 3rd ch of beg ch-3.

Rnds 8–18: Rep rnds 4–7 consecutively, ending with rnd 6. At end of rnd 18, fasten off MC.

Rnd 19: With size C [E] hook, join CC with a sl st in first V-st sp, ch 3, 8 dc in same sp, *ch 1, dc in center dc of next 3-dc group, ch 1**, 9 dc in next V-st sp, rep from * around, ending last rep at **, join with sl st in 3rd ch of beg ch-3.

Rnd 20: Ch 1, sc in same st as joining, *[ch 4, sk next dc, sc in next dc] 4 times**, [sc in next sp, sc in next dc] twice, rep from * around, ending last rep at **, sc in next sp, sc in next dc, sc in next sp, join with sl st in beg sc. Fasten off.

Sleeve
Make 2.

Rnd 1: With size B [D] hook, join CC with a sl st in 5th ch from the right on ch-8 at bottom of either armhole, ch 1, sc in same st, ch 2, sk 2 ch, sc in next ch; working in rem lps of 27 sk sts on row 10 of Yoke, ch 2, sk first st, sc in next st, [ch 2, sk 2 sts, sc in next st, ch 2, sk next st, sc in next st] 5 times, ch 2, sk first 2 ch of ch-8, sc in next ch, ch 2, join with sl st in beg sc. *(14 ch-2 sps)*

Rnd 2: Sl st in first sp, ch 3, 4 dc in same sp, dc in next sp, [5 dc in next sp, dc in next sp] around, join with sl st in 3rd ch of beg ch-3.

Rnd 3: (Sl st, ch 3) in next dc, dc in each of next 2 dc, *sk next dc, V-st in next dc**, dc in each of 3 center dc of next 5-dc group, rep from * around, ending last rep at **, join

with sl st in 3rd ch of beg ch-3.

Rnd 4: (Sl st, ch 3) in next dc, *5 dc in next V-st sp**, dc in center dc of next 3-dc group, rep from * around, ending last rep at **, join with sl st in 3rd ch of beg ch-3.

Rnd 5: Beg V-st in same st as joining, *dc in each of 3 center dc of next 5-dc group**, sk next dc, V-st in next dc, rep from * around, ending last rep at **, join with sl st in 3rd ch of beg ch-5.

Rnd 6: Sl st in V-st sp, ch 3, 4 dc in same sp, *sc in center dc of next 3-dc group**, 5 dc in next V-st sp, rep from * around, ending last rep at **, join with sl st in 3rd ch of beg ch-3. Fasten off.

Neck Trim

With size B [D] hook, RS facing, join CC with a sl st in corner st at left back neck opening, ch 1, working in rem lps of foundation ch across, sc in same st, sk 2 sts, [3 dc in next st, sk next st, sc in next st] across. Fasten off.

Finishing

Beg at center front, weave length of 1-inch-wide ribbon through sps of rnd 1 of Skirt. Tie in bow at front.

With sewing needle and thread, sew hook-and-loop fastener at back opening of dress. With sewing needle and thread, sew lace appliqué at center front of dress Yoke. Sew 1 paper rose at center of appliqué.

BOOTIE
Make 2.
Sole

Rnd 1: With size B [D] hook, beg at heel with MC, ch 18, dc in 4th ch from hook, 2 dc in next ch, dc in each of next 12 chs, 5 dc in last ch for toe; working in rem lps across opposite side of foundation ch, dc in each of next 12 chs, 2 dc in next ch, join with sl st in last ch of ch-18. *(35 dc)*

Rnd 2: Ch 2 *(counts as first hdc throughout)*, 2 hdc in each of next 3 dc, hdc in each of next 11 dc, 2 hdc in each of next 6 dc, hdc in each of next 11 dc, 2 hdc in each of next 3 dc, join with sl st in 2nd ch of beg ch-2. *(47 hdc)*

Rnd 3: Ch 2, [2 hdc in next hdc, hdc in next hdc] 3 times, hdc in each of next 11 hdc, [2 hdc in next hdc, hdc in next hdc] 6 times, hdc in each of next 11 hdc, [2 hdc in next hdc, hdc in next hdc] 3 times, join with sl st in 2nd ch of beg ch-2. *(59 hdc)*

Sides

Rnd 1: Ch 1, **bpsc** *(see Special Stitches)* over each hdc around, join with sl st in front lp only of first bpsc. Turn.

Rnds 2–4: Ch 1, sc in same st as joining, sc in each rem sc around, join with sl st in first sc, turn. At end of rnd 4, fasten off.

Instep

Row 1: With RS facing, counting joining sc at end of last rnd of Sides as first st, count 25 sc to the left of heel, join CC with sl st in back lp only of next sc, ch 1, sc in same sc, sc in back lp only of each of next 9 sc across toe, turn. *(10 sc)*

Rows 2–9: Ch 1, sc in each sc across, turn. Do not fasten off at end of row 9.

Connect Instep to Bootie

With heel of Bootie facing, counting joining sc at end of last rnd of Sides as first st, count 16 sts to left of heel and place marker in 16th st; count 16 sts to right of heel and place 2nd marker in 16th st.

With lp still on hook, insert hook in marked st on same side of Bootie where last row of instep ended, complete sc; working towards toe through both thicknesses of Instep and Sides at the same time, sc in each rem lp across base of Instep; working through both thicknesses, sc up opposite side of Instep, ending in rem marked st. Do not fasten off.

Top

Rnd 1: Ch 4 *(counts as first dc, ch-1)*; working toward heel, dc in first unworked sc, ch 1, [sk next unworked sc, dc in next unworked sc, ch 1] 14 times; working across 10 sts at top of Instep, dc in first sc, ch 1, [sk next sc, dc in next sc, ch 1] 4 times, join with sl st in 4th ch of beg ch-4. Do not turn. *(21 ch-1 sps)*

Row 2: Ch 1, sc in same st as joining, *ch 4, [sc, ch 4] 3 times in next sp, sc in next dc, rep from * across to corresponding st on opposite side of Instep. Do not work across top of Instep. Turn.

Rows 3 & 4: Sl st in first sp, ch 1, sc in same sp, ch 4, [sc in next sp, ch 4] across. Turn.

At end of row 4, fasten off.

Finishing

Beg at center front, weave length of 1-inch-wide ribbon through sps of rnd 1 of Bootie Top on each Bootie. Tie in bow at front.

With sewing needle and thread, sew 1 rose at center of Instep on each Bootie. ❏❏

Morning Glory

SKILL LEVEL

INTERMEDIATE

FINISHED SIZES
Fits 17-inch chest *(6 months)* [18-inch chest *(12 months)*]
Pattern is written for smaller size with changes for larger size in brackets. When only 1 number is given, it applies to both sizes.

FINISHED MEASUREMENT
Chest: 18 [19] inches

MATERIALS
6 months
❏ Red Heart Soft Baby fine (sport) weight yarn (7 oz/594 yds/198g per skein):
   1 skein each MC and CC
❏ Size B/1/2.25mm and C/2/2.75mm crochet hooks or sizes needed to obtain gauge
12 months
❏ Bernat Softee Baby fine (sport) weight yarn (5 oz/455 yds/140g per skein):
   1 skein each MC and CC
❏ Size D/3/3.25mm and E/4/3.5mm crochet hooks or sizes needed to obtain gauge
Both sizes
❏ Sewing needle
❏ 2 yds 1-inch-wide ribbon
❏ 6 heart-shaped ⁷⁄₁₆-inch buttons
❏ 8 satin 1¼-inch roses with leaves
❏ White sewing thread

GAUGE
Size B hook and Red Heart Soft Baby: 25 dc = 5 inches
Size D hook and Bernat Softee Baby: 23 dc = 5 inches

SPECIAL STITCHES
Left shell: (Dc, ch 2, 3 dc) in indicated st or sp.
Beginning left shell (beg left shell): (Ch 5, 3 dc) in indicated st or sp.
Right shell: (3 dc, ch 2, dc) in indicated st or sp.

Beginning right shell (beg right shell): (Ch 3, 2 dc, ch 2, dc) in indicated st or sp.
Shell: (3 dc, ch 4, 3 dc) in indicated st or sp.
Beginning shell (beg shell): (Ch 3, 2 dc, ch 4, 3 dc) in indicated st or sp.
V-stitch (V-st): (Dc, ch 3, dc) in indicated st or sp.
Cluster (cl): Holding back on hook last lp of each st, dc in each of next 3 indicated dc, yo, draw through all 4 lps on hook.
Beginning cluster (beg cl): Ch 2; holding back on hook last lp of each st, dc in each of next 2 dc, yo, draw through all 3 lps on hook.
Bobble: Holding back on hook last lp of each st, 3 dc in indicated st or sp, yo, draw through all 4 lps on hook.
Beginning bobble (beg bobble): Ch 2; holding back on hook last lp of each st, 2 dc in same st as ch-2, yo, draw through all 3 lps on hook.

INSTRUCTIONS
DRESS
Yoke
Row 1: Beg at neck, with size B [D] hook and CC, ch 63, sc in 2nd ch from hook, sc in each rem ch across, turn. *(62 sc)*
Row 2: Ch 3 *(counts as first dc throughout)*, dc in each of next 6 sc, 5 dc in next sc *(corner made)*, dc in each of next 16 sc, 5 dc in next sc *(corner made)*, dc in each of next 12 sc, 5 dc in next sc *(corner made)*, dc in each of next 16 sc, 5 dc in next sc *(corner made)*, dc in each of last 7 sc, turn. *(78 dc)*
Row 3: Ch 1, sc in each dc around, working 3 sc in center dc of each corner, turn. *(86 sc)*
Row 4: Ch 3, dc in each sc around, working 5 dc in center sc of each corner, turn. *(102 dc)*
Rows 5–10: Rep rows 3 and 4 alternately. *(174 dc at end of row 10)*
Row 11: Ch 1, sc in each of first 21 dc, 2 sc in next sc, ch 1, sk next 44 dc for armhole, sc in each of next 42 dc, ch 1, sk next 44 dc for armhole,

2 sc in next dc, sc in each of last 21 dc, turn.
Row 12: Ch 4 *(counts as first tr)*, tr in next sc, [ch 1, sk next sc, tr in each of next 2 sc] across to first ch-1 sp, ch 1, sk ch-1 sp, [tr in each of next 2 sc, ch 1, sk next sc] across to last sc before next ch-1 sp, sk last sc before sp and ch-1 sp, tr in each of next 2 sc, [ch 1, sk next sc, tr in each of next 2 sc] across, turn. *(30 pairs of tr)*
Row 13: Ch 1, sc in each tr and 2 sc in each ch-1 sp across. Fasten off CC. Turn. *(118 sc)*

Skirt
Row 1: With size C [E] hook, join MC with a sl st in first sc, ch 1, sc in same sc, ch 3, sk 2 sc, sc in next sc, [(ch 3, sk next sc, sc in next sc) 8 times, ch 3, sk 2 sc, sc in next sc] across, turn. *(55 ch-3 sps)*
Row 2: (Sl st, ch 1, sc) in first ch-3 sp, [ch 4, sc in next sp] across, turn. *(54 ch-4 sps)*
Rnd 3: Sl st in first sp, **beg left shell** *(see Special Stitches)* in same sp, **left shell** *(see Special Stitches)* in each rem sp around, join with sl st in 3rd ch of beg ch-5. *(54 shells)*
Rnd 4: Sl st in left shell sp, **beg right shell** *(see Special Stitches)* in same sp, **right shell** *(see Special Stitches)* in each rem shell sp around, join with sl st in 3rd ch of beg ch-3.
Rnd 5: Sl st in each of next 2 dc and in shell sp, beg left shell in same sp, left shell in each rem shell sp around, join with sl st in 3rd ch of beg ch-5.
Rnds 6–13: Rep rnds 4 and 5 alternately. At end of rnd 13, fasten off MC.

Edging
Rnd 1: With C [E] hook, join CC with a sl st in any shell sp, **beg shell** *(see Special Stitches)* in same sp, *ch 1, **V-st** *(see Special Stitches)* in next shell sp, ch 1**, **shell** *(see Special Stitches)* in next shell sp, rep from * around, ending last rep at **, join with sl st in 3rd ch of beg ch-3.
Rnd 2: Sl st in each of next 2 dc, (sl st, ch 3, 8 dc) in next shell sp, ch

1, *V-st in next V-st sp, ch 1**, 9 dc in next shell sp, rep from * around, ending last rep at **, join with sl st in 3rd ch of beg ch-3.

Rnd 3: Beg cl (see Special Stitches) over same st as joining and next 2 dc, *[ch 4, cl (see Special Stitches) over next 3 dc] twice, ch 1, (**bobble** {see Special Stitches}, ch 3, bobble) in next V-st sp, ch 1**, cl over first 3 dc of next 9-dc group, rep from * around, ending last rep at **, join with sl st in top of beg cl.

Rnd 4: (Sl st, ch 1, 7 sc) in first sp, *ch 4, 7 sc in next sp, sc in next ch-1 sp, 7 sc in next sp, sc in next ch-1 sp**, 7 sc in next sp, rep from * around, ending last rep at **, join with sl st in beg sc. Fasten off.

Neck & Front Opening Edging

Rnd 1: With size B [D] hook, join CC with a sl st in corner at left front neck opening, ch 1, 2 sc in same st, sc evenly spaced over ends of rows down to bottom of front opening, sc evenly spaced over ends of rows up to right neck corner, sc evenly spaced around neck opening, sc in same st as first sc, join with sl st in beg sc, turn.

Row 2: Ch 1, 2 sc in same sc as joining, sc around, working 3 sc in center sc of 3-sc corner group, sc in same sc as first sc, join with sl st in beg sc, turn.

Row 3: Working over front opening only, ch 1, sc in same sc as last sc, sc down to bottom of front opening, sc up front opening to next corner, working (ch 2, sc in next sc) 4 times evenly spaced for buttonholes, ending with sc in center sc of 3-sc corner group. Fasten off.

Sleeve
Make 2.

Rnd 1: With size B [D] hook, join CC with a sl st in ch-1 sp at bottom of either armhole, ch 1, sc in same

sp, ch 3, sc in first unworked sc of row 10 of yoke, [ch 3, sk 2 sc, sc in next sc] across, ending with ch 3, sk last sc, join with sl st in beg sc. (16 ch-3 sps)

Rnd 2: Sl st in first sp, ch 1, sc in same sp, 5 dc in next sp, [sc in next sp, 5 dc in next sp] around, join with sl st in beg sc.

Rnd 3: Sl st in each of next 2 dc, (sl st, ch 3, 4 dc) in next dc, 5 dc in center dc of each 5-dc group around, join with sl st in 3rd ch of beg ch-3.

Rnd 4: Sl st in next dc, (sl st, **beg bobble** {see Special Stitches}) in next dc, *ch 4, sc between same 5-dc group and next 5-dc group, ch 4**, bobble in center dc of next 5-dc group, rep from * around, ending last rep at **, join with sl st in top of beg bobble. Fasten off.
Rep on rem armhole.

Finishing

With sewing needle and sewing thread, sew buttons onto left front Yoke opposite buttonholes.

Beg at front opening, weave ribbon through sps on rnd 12 of Yoke. Tie in bow at center front. Using photo as a guide, tack 3 roses onto each side of front Yoke.

BOOTIE
Make 2.

Rnd 1: With size B [D] hook and MC, beg at heel, ch 16, 2 sc in 2nd ch from hook, sc in each of next 13 ch, 3 sc in last ch (toe); working in rem lps across opposite side of foundation ch, sc in each of next 13 ch, sc in same ch as first sc, join with sl st in beg sc. (32 sc)

Rnd 2: Ch 1, 2 sc in same sc as joining, 2 sc in next sc, sc in each of next 13 sc, 2 sc in each of next 3 sc, sc in each of next 13 sc, 2 sc in last sc, join with sl st in beg sc. (38 sc)

Rnd 3: Ch 1; beg in same sc as joining,

sc in each sc around, working 3 sc evenly spaced across toe and heel, join with sl st in beg sc. (44 sc)

Rnds 4–6: Rep rnd 3. (62 sc at end of rnd 6)

Rnd 7: Ch 1, sc in same sc as joining, sc in each rem sc around, join with sl st in beg sc.

Rnd 8: Ch 1, sc in same sc as joining, sc in each rem sc around, working **sc dec** (see Stitch Guide) in 2 sc evenly spaced twice at toe, join with sl st in beg sc. (60 sts)

Rnd 9: Rep rnd 8. (58 sts)

Rnd 10: Ch 1; beg in same sc as joining, sc in each rem st around, working sc dec in 2 sts evenly spaced twice at toe and twice at heel, join with sl st in first sc. (54 sts)

Rnds 11–15: Rep rnds 9 and 10 alternately, ending with rnd 9. At end of rnd 15, fasten off. (40 sts at end of rnd 15)

Strap
Make 2.

With size B [D] hook and MC, ch 16, sc in 2nd ch from hook, sk next ch for buttonhole, sc in each rem ch across. Fasten off, leaving length for finishing. Count 13 sts to the right of heel center and sew strap in place using length left for finishing on first Bootie. For rem Bootie, count 13 sts to the left of heel center and sew strip in place.

Edging

With size B [D] hook, join CC with a sl st at heel, ch 1, sc in same sc, sc around entire Bootie top including Strap, working 3 sc in st at top of Strap, join with sl st in beg sc. Fasten off.

Finishing

With sewing needle and thread, sew buttons onto Booties. Tack 1 rose onto center front of each Bootie. ❏❏

Rose Petals

FINISHED SIZE
Fits 17-inch chest (3–6 months)

FINISHED MEASUREMENT
Chest: 19 inches

MATERIALS
- ❏ Size 10 crochet cotton:
  4000 yds white
- ❏ Size 0/2.5mm steel crochet hook or size needed to obtain gauge
- ❏ Sewing needle
- ❏ 4 yds ¼-inch-wide pink ribbon
- ❏ White sewing thread

GAUGE
First Rose = 1¾ inches in diameter with 2 strands held tog

PATTERN NOTE
Sweater, Bonnet and Booties are worked with 2 strands held together as 1 throughout.

SPECIAL STITCHES
Shell: 5 dc in **back lp** (see Stitch Guide) only of indicated st.

Half shell: 3 dc in back lp only of indicated st.

Beginning half shell (beg half shell): (Ch 3, 2 dc) in back lp only of indicated st.

Picot: Ch 3, sc in 3rd ch from hook.

Small shell (sm shell): 3 dc in back lp only of indicated st.

Back post single crochet (bpsc): Insert hook from back to front to back around **post** (see Stitch Guide) of indicated st, yo, draw up a lp, complete sc.

INSTRUCTIONS
SWEATER
Rose Yoke
First Rose
Rnd 1 (RS): Ch 5, join with sl st to form ring, ch 1, 10 sc in ring, join with sl st in first sc. (10 sc)

Rnd 2: Ch 1, sc in same sc as joining, [5 dc in next sc, sc in next sc] 4 times, 5 dc in next sc, join with sl st in first sc. Fasten off. (5 petals)

2nd Rose
Rnd 1: Rep rnd 1 of First Rose.

Rnd 2: Ch 1, sc in same sc as joining, 2 dc in next sc, remove hook from lp, insert hook in 4th dc made on last petal of previous Rose, *pick up dropped lp, draw through st on hook, ch 1, 3 dc in same sc on working motif as last 2 dc worked* (first petal joined), sc in next sc on working motif, 2 dc in next sc, remove hook from lp, sk next sc and next dc on previous motif, insert hook in next dc, rep from * to * (2nd petal joined), continue around as for rnd 2 of First Rose.

Remaining 11 Roses
Rnd 1: Rep rnd 1 of First Rose.

Rnd 2: Ch 1, sc in same sc as joining, 2 dc in next sc, remove hook from lp, insert hook in 4th dc made on 4th petal of previous Rose, *pick up dropped lp, draw through st on hook, ch 1, 3 dc in same sc on working motif as last 2 dc worked* (first petal joined), sc in next sc on working motif, 2 dc in next sc, remove hook from lp, sk next sc and next dc on 3rd petal of previous motif, insert hook in next dc, rep from * to * (2nd petal joined), continue around as for rnd 2 of First Rose. There will be no free petals between joined petals on 1 edge of Rose Yoke (neck edge) and 1 free petal between joined petals on opposite side of Rose Yoke (body edge).

Neck Trim
Row 1: With RS facing, join yarn with a sl st in 4th dc from the right on first free petal to the right of joined petal on neck edge of Rose Yoke, ch 1, sc in same st, *ch 5, sk next dc, next sc and next dc, sc in next dc on next petal of same Rose**, ch 5, sc in 4th dc on next petal of next rose, rep from * across to last Rose, ending last rep at **. Turn. (25 sps)

Row 2: Sl st in first sp, ch 6 (counts as first dc, ch-3), dc in next sp, [ch 3, dc in next sp] across. Fasten off.

Body
Row 1: With RS facing, working across body edge of Rose Yoke, join thread with a sl st in center dc of 4th petal of end Rose, ch 1, sc in same dc, *ch 5, sc in next sc, ch 5, sc in center dc of next petal of same Rose, ch 5, sc in next sc**, ch 5, sc in joining between same Rose and next Rose, rep from * across to last Rose, ending last rep at **, ch 2, dc in center dc of last unworked petal of last Rose, turn. (52 ch-5 sps)

Row 2: Ch 1, sc in lp just formed, [**shell** (see Special Stitches) in next sc, sc in next sp] across, turn. (51 shells)

Row 3: Beg half shell (see Special Stitches) in first sc, sc in center dc of next shell, [shell in next sc, sc in center dc of next shell] across to last shell, **half shell** (see Special Stitches) in last sc, turn. (50 shells, 2 half shells)

Row 4: Ch 1, sc in first dc, shell in next sc, [sc center dc of next shell, shell in next sc] across to last sc, sc in 3rd ch of beg ch-3, turn. (51 shells)

Row 5: Beg half shell in first sc, [sc in center dc of next shell, shell in next sc] 6 times, sc in center dc of next shell, sk next 11 shells for first armhole, sc in center dc of next shell, [shell in next sc, sc in center dc of next shell] 14 times, sk next 11 shells for 2nd armhole, sc in center dc of next shell, [shell in next sc, sc in center dc of next shell] 6 times, half shell in last sc, turn. (26 shells, 2 half shells)

Row 6: Ch 1, sc in first dc, [shell in next sc, sc in center dc of next shell] 6 times, shell in next sc at base of armhole, sc in center dc of next shell, [shell in next sc, sc in center dc of next shell] 13 times, shell in next sc at base of armhole, [sc in center dc of next shell, shell in next sc] 6 times, sc in 3rd ch of beg ch-3, turn. (27 shells)

Row 7: Beg half shell in first sc, [sc in center dc of next shell, shell in next sc] 5 times, *(sc, dc, sc) in center

dc of next shell, shell in next sc*, sc in center dc of next shell, shell in next sc, rep from * to *, [sc in center dc of next shell, shell in next sc] 11 times, rep from * to *, sc in center dc of next shell, shell in next sc, rep from * to *, [sc in center dc of next shell, shell in next sc] 4 times, sc in center dc of next shell, half shell in last sc, turn.

Row 8: Ch 1, sc in first dc, *[shell in next sc, sc in center dc of next shell] across to next (sc, dc, sc) group, shell in first sc, sc in next dc, shell in next sc, sc in center dc of next shell**, rep from * across to last (sc, dc, sc) group, ending last rep at **, shell in next sc, [sc in center dc of next shell, shell in next sc] across to last sc, sc in 3rd ch of beg ch-3, turn. *(31 shells)*

Row 9: Beg half shell in first sc, sc in center dc of next shell, [shell in next sc, sc in center dc of next shell] across, ending with half shell in last sc, turn. *(30 shells, 2 half shells)*

Row 10: Ch 1, sc in first dc, shell in next sc, [sc in center dc of next shell, shell in next sc] across, ending with sc in 3rd ch of beg ch-3, turn. *(31 shells)*

Rows 11–22: Rep rows 9 and 10 alternately. At end of row 22, fasten off.

Sleeve
Make 2.
Rnd 1: With RS facing, join thread with a sl st in joining st at bottom of either armhole, ch 1, sc in same st, shell in next sc, [sc in center dc of next shell, shell in next sc] around, join with sl st in beg sc, sl st in each of next 3 dc, turn. *(12 shells)*

Rnd 2: Ch 1, sc in same dc as last sl st, shell in joining st, [sc in center dc of next shell, shell in next sc] around, join with sl st in first sc, sl st in each of next 3 dc, turn.

Rep rnd 2 until sleeve measures 6½ inches or desired length, ending with a WS rnd. At end of last rnd, join with sl st in beg sc. Do not fasten off. Turn.

Cuff
Rnd 1: Sl st in each of first 2 dc, ch 1, sc in same st as last sl st and in each of next 2 dc, dc in each of 3 center dc of each shell around, join with sl st in **front lp** *(see Stitch Guide)* only

of beg sc, turn. *(36 sc)*

Rnd 2: Ch 1; working in back lps only this rnd, sc in each sc around, join with sl st in front lp only of beg sc, turn.

Rnds 3 & 4: Rep rnd 2.

Rnd 5: Ch 1, sc in same sc as joining, *picot *(see Special Stitches)*, sk next st**, sc in next st, rep from * around, ending last rep at **, join with sl st in beg sc. Fasten off.

Rep on rem armhole.

Yoke Edging
With RS facing, join thread with sl st over end sp of row 1 of Body, ch 1, sc in same st, picot, sc in 4th petal on last Rose of Rose Yoke, picot, sc in next sc on Rose, picot, sk next dc, sc in next dc on Rose, [picot, sc in end sp on next row of Neck Trim] twice, picot, sc in top of first st on row 2 of Neck Trim; working across top of row 2 of Neck Trim, [picot, sc in next dc] across to last dc, picot, sc over end sp of row 2, picot, sc over end sp of next row, picot, sc in 4th dc on next petal of end Rose on Rose Yoke, picot, sc in next sc, picot, sk next dc, sc in next dc, picot, sc over end sp of row 1 of Body. Fasten off.

Finishing
Weave length of ribbon through sps of row 2 of Neck Trim on Sweater.

BONNET
Center Back
First Rose
Rep instructions for First Rose for Sweater.

2nd Rose
Rep instructions for 2nd Rose for Sweater.

3rd Rose
Rnd 1: Rep rnd 1 for First Rose for Sweater.

Rnd 2: Ch 1, sc in same sc as joining, 3 dc in next sc, remove hook from lp, insert hook in 2nd dc made on first petal of First Rose, *pick up dropped lp, draw through st on hook, ch 1, 2 dc in same sc on working motif as last 3 dc worked* (first petal joined), sc in next sc on working motif, 3 dc in next sc, remove hook from lp,

insert hook in joining between First and 2nd Rose, pick up dropped lp, draw through to RS, 2 dc in same sc as last 3 dc made, sc in next sc, 2 dc in next sc, remove hook from lp, insert hook in 4th dc on 5th petal of 2nd Rose, pick up dropped lp, draw through st on hook, 3 dc in same sc as last 2 dc made, sc in next sc, continue around as for rnd 2 of First Rose. Do not fasten off.

Back
Rnd 1: Ch 1, sc in same sc as joining, *ch 5, sc in joining between same Rose and next Rose, ch 5, sc in next sc on next Rose**, [ch 5, sc in center dc of next petal on same Rose, ch 5, sc in next sc on same Rose] twice, rep from * around, ending last rep at **, ch 5, sc in center dc of next petal on same Rose, ch 5, sc in next sc on same Rose, ch 5, sc in center dc of next petal on same Rose, ch 2, dc in first sc to form last ch-5 sp, turn. *(18 ch-5 sps)*

Rnd 2: Ch 1, sc in sp just formed, [ch 5, sc in next sp] around, ending with ch 2, dc in first sc to form last ch-5 sp, turn.

Rnd 3: Ch 1, sc in sp just formed, shell in next sc, [sc in next sp, shell in next sc] around, join with sl st in first sc, sl st in each of next 3 dc, turn. *(18 shells)*

Rnd 4: Ch 1, sc in same st as last sl st made, shell in joining sl st, [sc in center dc of next shell, shell in next sc] around, join with sl st in first sc, sl st in each of next 3 dc, turn.

Rnds 5–7: Rep rnd 4. At end of rnd 7, join with sl st in beg sc, turn. Do not fasten off.

Sides
Row 1: Beg half shell in same sc as joining, [sc in center dc of next shell, shell in next sc] 13 times, sc in center dc of next shell, half shell in next sc, leave rem 4 shells unworked, turn. *(13 shells, 2 half shells)*

Row 2: Ch 1, sc in first dc, shell in next sc, [sc in center dc of next shell, shell in next sc] across, sc in 3rd ch of beg ch-3, turn. *(14 shells)*

Row 3: Beg half shell in first sc, sc in center dc of next shell, [shell in next sc, sc in center dc of next shell] across, half shell in last sc, turn.

Rows 4–9: Rep rows 2 and 3 alternately.

Row 10: Ch 1, sc in first dc, ch 6, sc in next sc, [ch 6, sc in center dc of next shell, ch 6, sc in next sc] across to last sc, ch 3, dc in 3rd ch of beg ch-3 to form last ch-6 sp. *(28 ch-6 sps)*

Row 11: Ch 1, sc in sp just formed, [shell in next sc, sc in next sp] across, turn. *(27 shells)*

Row 12: Rep row 3. Do not fasten off.

Neck Edging

Row 1: Working over end sts of last 12 rows and skipping sts as necessary to tighten edge slightly, sc evenly spaced across to last rnd of Back, sc in each of 3 center dc of each unworked shell across last rnd of Back, sc evenly spaced over end sts of Sides to top of last row of Sides, turn.

Rows 2–4: Ch 1; working in back lps only, sc in each sc across, turn. At end of row 4, fasten off.

Finishing

Weave length of ribbon through sps on row 10 of Bonnet.

BOOTIE
Make 2.
Sole

Rnd 1: Beg at heel, ch 18, dc in 4th ch from hook, 2 dc in next ch, dc in each of next 12 ch, 5 dc in last ch; working in rem lps across opposite side of foundation ch, dc in each of next 12 ch, 2 dc in next ch, join with sl st in last ch of ch-18. *(35 dc)*

Rnd 2: Ch 3 *(counts as first dc throughout)*, 2 dc in each of next 3 dc, dc in each of next 11 dc, 2 dc in each of next 6 dc, dc in each of next 11 dc, 2 dc in each of next 3 dc, join with sl st in 3rd ch of beg ch-3. *(47 dc)*

Rnd 3: Ch 3, [2 dc in next dc, dc in next dc] 3 times, dc in each of next 11 dc, [2 dc in next dc, dc in next dc] 6 times, dc in each of next 11 dc, [2 dc in next dc, dc in next dc] 3 times, join with sl st in 3rd ch of beg ch-3. *(59 dc)*

Body

Rnd 1: Ch 1; beg in same st as joining, **bpsc** *(see Special Stitches)* over each dc around, join with sl st in first bpsc.

Rnds 2–7: Ch 1; working in back lps only, sc in same st as joining, sc in each rem sc around, join with sl st in first sc. At end of rnd 7, fasten off.

Instep

Row 1: Fold Bootie in half to find center st at toe end; with WS facing, count 5 sts to the right of center st; join thread with a sl st in front lp only of next st, ch 1, sc in same st; working in front lps only this row, sc in each of next 10 sts, turn. *(11 sc)*

Rows 2–10: Ch 1; working in back lps only, sc in each sc across, turn. At end of row 10, do not fasten off.

Join Instep to Body

Mark 10th unworked st on each side of rnd 7 of Body from first and last sts of row 1 of Instep. Working through both thicknesses at once and easing to fit, sc in each of next 10 sts, sc in each rem lp across toe at base of row 1 of Instep; working through both thicknesses at once and easing to fit, sc in each of next 10 sts. Do not fasten off. Do not turn.

Bootie Top

Rnd 1: Ch 4 *(counts as first dc, ch-1)*; working across top of Instep, dc in first sc on last row of Instep, [ch 1, sk next sc, dc in next sc] 5 times; working around rem unworked sts of rnd 7 of body, ch 1, dc in same sc on Body as Instep joining st, ch 1, [sk next st, dc in next st, ch 1] around, join with sl st in 3rd ch of beg ch-4. Turn. *(22 ch-1 sps)*

Rnd 2: Ch 1, sc in same st as joining, [ch 5, sk next dc, sc in next dc] around, ending ch 2, dc in first sc to form last ch-5 sp, turn. *(11 ch-5 sps)*

Rnd 3: Ch 1, sc in sp just formed, **sm shell** *(see Special Stitches)* in next sc, [sc in next sp, sm shell in next sc] around, join with sl st in beg sc, sl st in each of next 2 dc, turn. *(11 sm shells)*

Rnds 4–7: Ch 1, sc in same st as last sl st made, sm shell in joining sl st, [sc in center dc of next sm shell, sm shell in next sc] around, join with sl st in beg sc, sl st in each of next 2 dc, turn. At end of rnd 7, join with sl st in first sc, fasten off.

Finishing

Weave length of ribbon through sps on rnd 1 of Bootie Top. ❏❏

SKILL LEVEL

INTERMEDIATE

FINISHED SIZES

Fits 17-inch chest *(6 months)* [18-inch chest *(12 months)*]
Pattern is written for smaller size with changes for larger size in brackets. When only 1 number is given, it applies to both sizes.

FINISHED MEASUREMENT

Chest: 19 [20] inches

MATERIALS

❑ Bernat Softee Baby fine (sport) weight yarn (5 oz/455 yds/ 140g per skein):
    2 skeins
❑ Size B/1/2.25mm [D/3/3.25] and C/2/2.75mm [E/4/3.5mm] crochet hooks or sizes needed to obtain gauge
❑ Embroidery needle
❑ Sewing needle
❑ 2 yds 1-inch-wide ribbon
❑ 2 yds ⅜-inch-wide ribbon
❑ 7 pearl ¼-inch shank buttons
❑ Hook-and-loop fasteners
❑ 6-strand embroidery floss:
    1 skein each of 2 colors for flowers *(MC and CC)*
    1 skein green for leaves
❑ White sewing thread

GAUGE

Size B hook: 10 hdc = 2 inches
Size D hook: 9 hdc = 2 inches

SPECIAL STITCHES

Long double crochet (ldc): Yo, insert hook in indicated st, yo, draw up a lp to ½ inch, [yo, draw through 2 lps on hook] twice.
V-stitch (V-st): (Dc, ch 3, dc) in indicated st or sp.
Beginning V-stitch (beg V-st): (Ch 6, dc) in indicated st or sp.
Shell: (Sc, hdc, dc, hdc, sc) in indicated st or sp.
Large shell (lg shell): (Sc, hdc, 2 dc, hdc, sc) in indicated st or sp.
Bobble: Holding back on hook last

lp of each st, tr 3 times in indicated st or sp, yo, draw through all 4 lps on hook.

INSTRUCTIONS

FLOWER
Make 4 MC.
Make 1 CC.

With size B hook and embroidery floss, ch 4, join with sl st to form ring, ch 1, (sc, ch 3, **bobble** *{see Special Stitches}*, ch 3) 5 times in ring, join with sl st in first sc. Fasten off, leaving short length for finishing.

Leaf
Make 11.

With size B hook and green embroidery floss, ch 5, sc in 2nd ch from hook, hdc in next ch, dc in next ch, 5 dc in last ch; working in rem lps across opposite side of foundation ch, dc in next ch, hdc in next ch, sc in same ch as first sc, join with sl st in beg sc. Fasten off, leaving short length for finishing.

DRESS
Yoke
Row 1: Beg at neck with size B [D] hook, ch 59, sc in 2nd ch from hook, sc in each rem ch across, turn. *(58 sc)*
Row 2: Ch 1, sc in each of first 9 sc, 3 sc in next sc *(corner made),* sc in each of next 9 sc, 3 sc in next sc *(corner made),* sc in each of next 18 sc, [3 sc in next sc *(corner made),* sc in each of next 9 sc] twice, turn. *(66 sc)*
Row 3: Ch 2 *(counts as first hdc throughout),* hdc in each sc across, working 3 hdc in center sc of each 3-sc corner group, turn. *(74 hdc)*
Row 4: Ch 3 *(counts as first dc throughout),* **ldc** *(see Special Stitches)* in each hdc across, working 3 ldc in center hdc of each 3-hdc group around, turn. *(82 ldc)*
Row 5: Ch 2, hdc in each st across to center ldc of first 3-ldc corner group, 3 ldc in center ldc, sc in each st across to center hdc of next 3-hdc corner group, 3 hdc in center ldc, hdc in each st across to center ldc of next

3-ldc corner group, 3 hdc in center ldc, sc in each st across to center ldc of next 3-ldc corner group, 3 hdc in center ldc, hdc in each rem hdc across, turn. *(60 hdc, 30 sc)*
Rows 6–10: Rep row 5. *(130 sts at end of row 10)*
Row 11: Ch 2, hdc in each of next 18 sts, *ch 8 for armhole, sk next 27 sts*, hdc in each of next 38 sts, rep from * to *, hdc in each of last 19 sts, turn. *(76 hdc)*
Row 12: Ch 2, hdc in each hdc and in each ch across, turn. *(92 hdc)*
Rnd 13: Ch 2, hdc in each of next 2 hdc, 2 hdc in next hdc, hdc in each of next 3 hdc, 2 hdc in next hdc, [hdc in each of next 4 hdc, 2 hdc in next hdc] 13 times, [hdc in each of next 3 hdc, 2 hdc in next hdc] 4 times, hdc in each of next 2 hdc, 2 hdc in last hdc, join with sl st in 2nd ch of beg ch-2. *(112 hdc)*

Skirt
Rnd 1: With size C [E] hook, ch 4 *(counts as first tr),* [tr in each of next 2 tr, ch 1, sk next tr] around, join with sl st in 4th ch of beg ch-4. *(75 tr)*
Rnd 2: Ch 1, sc in same st as joining, ch 2, [sk next st, sc in next st, ch 2] around, join with sl st in beg sc. *(56 ch-2 sps)*
Rnd 3: Sl st into first ch-2 sp, **beg V-st** *(see Special Stitches)* in same sp, **V-st** *(see Special Stitches)* in each sp around, join with sl st in 3rd ch of beg ch-6.
Rnd 4: Sl st into first V-st sp, (ch 1, **shell** *{see Special Stitches})* in same sp, shell in each V-st sp around, join with sl st in first sc.
Rnd 5: Sl st in next hdc, (sl st, beg V-st) in next dc, V-st in center dc of each shell around, join with sl st in 3rd ch of beg ch-6.
Rnds 6–12: Rep rnds 4 and 5 alternately, ending with rnd 4.
Rnd 13: Sl st in next hdc, (sl st, beg V-st) in next dc, ch 1, [V-st in center dc of next shell, ch 1] around, join with sl st in 3rd ch of beg ch-6.
Rnd 14: (Sl st, ch 1, shell) in first V-st st, sc in next ch-1 sp, [shell in next

V-st sp, sc in next ch-1 sp] around, join with sl st in beg sc.

Rnd 15: Sl st in next sc and next hdc, (sl st, beg V-st) in next dc, ch 1, [V-st in center dc of next shell, ch 1] around, join with sl st in 3rd ch of beg ch-6.

Rnds 16–19: Rep rnds 14 and 15 alternately.

Rnd 20: Sl st in first V-st sp, ch 1; beg in same sp, **lg shell** (see Special Stitches) in each V-st sp around, join with sl st in beg sc. Fasten off.

Sleeve
Make 2.
Rnd 1: With size B [D] hook, RS facing, join yarn with a sl st in 5th ch from right on ch-8 at either underarm, ch 1, sc in same ch, ch 3, sc in next ch, ch 3, sk next ch, sc in last ch, ch 3; working around 27 sk sc on row 10 of Yoke, sk first sc, sc in next sc, [ch 3, sk next sc, sc in next sc] 12 times, ch 3, sc in last sc, ch 3, sk first ch of ch-8, sc in next ch, ch 3, sk next ch, sc in next ch, ch 3, join with sl st in beg sc, turn. (19 ch-3 sps)

Row 2: (Sl st, ch 1, sc) in first sp, ch 4, [sc in next sp, ch 4] across to last sp, sc in last sp, turn. (18 ch-4 sps)

Rows 3–10: Rep row 2. (10 sps at end of row 10)

Rnd 11: Ch 1, sc in each of last 10 sps; working over end sps of rows, sk last row, sc over end sp of each of next 8 rows to bottom of armhole, sk first row; working up opposite side, sk first row, sc over end sp of each of next 8 rows, join with sl st in first sc. (26 sc)

Row 12: Ch 3, dc in each sc around, join with sl st in 3rd ch of beg ch-3.

Row 13: Ch 1, sc in same st as joining, ch 4, [sk next dc, sc in next dc, ch 4] around, join with sl st in beg sc. (13 ch-4 sps)

Row 14: Sl st in first sp, ch 1; beg in same sp, shell in each sp around, join with sl st in beg sc. Fasten off.

Neck Edging
Rnd 1: With size B [D] hook, RS facing, join yarn with a sl st at upper right neck corner at back opening, ch 1, sc in same st, sc evenly spaced down right back opening, sc evenly spaced up left back opening to left neck corner; working across neck opening, sc in corner, [ch 3, sk 2 sts, sc in next st] across to next corner, join with sl st in beg sc.

Rnd 2: Sl st in each sc down right back opening and up left back opening to first ch-3 sp at neck opening, shell in each ch-3 sp across neck opening, join with sl st in beg sl st. Fasten off.

Finishing
With sewing needle and sewing thread, sew hook-and-loop fasteners onto back dress opening.

With embroidery needle and lengths left for finishing, using photo as a guide, sew 3 Flowers and 7 Leaves onto front dress Yoke. With sewing needle and white sewing thread, sew 1 pearl button at center of each Flower on dress.

Beg at front opening, weave 1-inch-wide ribbon through sps on rnd 1 of Skirt. Tie in bow at center front. Weave length of ⅜-inch-wide ribbon through sps of rnd 13 of Sleeve.

BOOTIE
Make 2.
Rnd 1: Beg at heel, with size B [D] hook, ch 16, sc in 2nd ch from hook, sc in each of next 13 ch, 3 sc in last ch for toe; working in rem lps across opposite side of foundation ch, sc in each of next 13 ch, 2 sc in last ch, join with sl st in beg sc. (32 sc)

Rnd 2: Ch 1, 2 sc in same sc as joining, sc in each of next 13 sc, 2 sc in each of next 3 sc, sc in each of next 13 sc, 2 sc in each of last 2 sc, join with sl st in beg sc. (38 sc)

Rnds 3–6: Ch 1; beg in same sc as joining, sc in each sc around, inc 3 sc evenly spaced at heel and toe on each rnd, join with sl st in beg sc. (62 sc at end of rnd 6)

Rnd 7: Ch 1, sc in same sc as joining, sc in each rem sc around, join with sl st in beg sc.

Rnds 8 & 9: Ch 1, sc in same st as joining, sc in each rem st around, working 2 **sc decs** (see Stitch Guide) evenly spaced at toe, join with sl st in beg sc. (58 sts at end of rnd 9)

Rnd 10: Ch 1, sc in same st as joining, sc in each rem st around, working 2 sc decs evenly spaced at toe and 2 sc decs at heel, join with sl st in beg sc. (54 sts)

Rnd 11: Rep rnd 8. (52 sts)

Rnd 12: Rep rnd 10. (48 sts)

Rnds 13–15: Rep rnds 11 and 12 alternately, ending with rnd 11. At end of rnd 15, fasten off. (40 sts at end of rnd 15)

Strap
With size B [D] hook, ch 14, sc in 2nd ch from hook, sk next ch for buttonhole, sc in each rem ch across. Fasten off, leaving length for finishing. Count 13 sts to the right of heel center and sew strap in place using length left for finishing on first Bootie. For rem Bootie, count 13 sts to the left of heel center and sew strip in place.

Edging
With size B [D] hook, join yarn with a sl st at heel, ch 1, sc in same sc, sc around entire Bootie top including Strap, working 3 sc in st at top of Strap, join with sl st in beg sc. Fasten off.

Finishing
Sew buttons to Booties opposite buttonholes.

With embroidery needle and lengths left for finishing, using photo as a guide, sew 1 Flower and 2 Leaves on front of each Bootie. With sewing needle and white sewing thread, sew 1 pearl button at center of each Flower on Booties. ❑❑

Pink Parfait

FINISHED SIZES

Fits 16-inch chest *(newborn–3 months)* [17-inch chest *(6 months)*] Pattern is written for smaller size with changes for larger size in brackets. When only 1 number is given, it applies to both sizes.

FINISHED MEASUREMENT

Chest: 17 [18] inches

MATERIALS

Newborn–3 months

❑ Red Heart Soft Baby fine (sport) weight yarn (7 oz/594 yds/ 198g per skein):
   1 skein each MC and CC
❑ Size B/1/2.25mm and C/2/ 2.75mm crochet hooks or sizes needed to obtain gauge

6 months

❑ Bernat Softee Baby fine (sport) weight yarn (5 oz/455 yds/ 140g per skein):
   2 skeins MC and 1 skein CC
❑ Size D/3/3.25mm and E/4/3.5 crochet hooks or sizes needed to obtain gauge

Both sizes

❑ Sewing needle
❑ 3 yds 1-inch-wide sheer ribbon
❑ 2 buttons, ½-inch
❑ 5 satin 1-inch roses with leaves
❑ Sewing thread

GAUGE

Size B hook and Red Heart Soft Baby: 25 dc = 5 inches
Size D hook and Bernat Softee Baby: 23 dc = 5 inches

SPECIAL STITCHES

V-stitch (V-st): (Dc, ch 2, dc) in indicated st or sp.
Beginning V-stitch (beg V-st): (Ch 5, dc) in indicated st or sp.
Shell: (2 dc, ch 2, 2 dc) in indicated st or sp.
Back post single crochet (bpsc): Insert hook from back to front to

back around **post** *(see Stitch Guide)* of indicated st, yo, draw up a lp, complete sc.

INSTRUCTIONS

DRESS
Yoke

Row 1: With size B [D] hook and MC, ch 65, dc in 4th ch from hook, dc in each of next 10 ch, 3 dc in next ch *(corner made),* dc in each of next 5 ch, 3 dc in next ch *(corner made),* dc in each of next 25 ch, 3 dc in next ch *(corner made),* dc in each of next 5 ch, 3 dc in next ch *(corner made),* dc in each of last 12 ch, turn. *(71 dc)*

Row 2: Ch 3 *(counts as first dc through-out),* dc in each dc across, working 3 dc in center dc of each corner group, turn. *(79 dc)*

Row 3: Ch 3, dc in each dc across, working 5 dc in center dc of each corner group, turn. *(95 dc)*

Rows 4–6: Rep row 2. *(119 dc at end of row 6)*

Rnd 7: Ch 4 *(counts as first dc, ch-1),* sk 2 dc, dc in next dc, [ch 1, sk next dc, dc in next dc] 7 times, *ch 1, sk next dc, ({dc, ch 1} twice, dc) in next dc*, [ch 1, sk next dc, dc in next dc] 9 times, rep from * to *, [ch 1, sk next dc, dc in next dc] 19 times, rep from * to *, [ch 1, sk next dc, dc in next dc] 9 times, rep from * to *, [ch 1, sk next dc, dc in next dc] 8 times, ch 1, sk 2 dc, dc in last dc, join with sl st in 3rd ch of beg ch-4. Fasten off. *(66 ch-1 sps)*

Back Yoke

Row 1: Sk first 9 ch-1 sps to the right of joining; using size B [D] hook, join MC with a sl st in next dc to the right, ch 1, sc in same dc; working back towards joining, *2 sc in next sp, sc in next dc, [sc in next sp, sc in next dc] twice, 2 sc in next sp, sc in next dc*, sc in next sp, sc in next dc, rep from * to * once**, sc in next dc, rep from * to **, turn. *(46 sc)*

Row 2: Ch 1, sc in first sc, [ch 4, sk 2 sc, sc in next sc] across. Fasten off. *(15 ch-4 sps)*

Front Yoke

Row 1: Sk next 14 ch-1 sps on rnd 7 of Yoke; using size B [D] hook, join MC with a sl st in next dc, ch 1, sc in same dc, [2 sc in next sp, sc in next dc, (sc in next sp, sc in next dc) 3 times] 5 times, turn. *(46 sc)*

Row 2: Rep row 2 of Back Yoke.

Skirt

Rnd 1: With size C [E] hook, join MC with a sl st in 7th ch-4 sp from the right on Back Yoke, **beg V-st** *(see Special Stitches)* in same sp, [ch 2, **shell** *(see Special Stitches)* in next sp, ch 2, **V-st** *(see Special Stitches)* in next sp] 4 times, ch 5 for underarm, V-st in next ch-4 sp on Front Yoke, [ch 2, shell in next sp, ch 2, V-st in next sp] 7 times, ch 5 for underarm, V-st in next ch-4 sp on Back Yoke, ch 2, shell in next sp, [ch 2, V-st in next sp, ch 2, shell in next sp] twice, ch 2, join with sl st in 3rd ch of beg ch-5

Rnd 2: (Sl st, beg V-st) in first V-st sp, *[ch 2, shell in next shell sp, ch 2, V-st in next V-st sp] across to ch-5, ch 2, shell in center ch of ch-5, ch 2, V-st in next V-st sp*, rep from * to *, ch 2, shell in next shell sp, ch 2, [V-st st in next V-st sp, ch 2, shell in next shell sp, ch 2] around, join with sl st in 3rd ch of beg ch-5.

Rnds 3–5: (Sl st, beg V-st) in first V-st sp, ch 2, shell in next shell sp, ch 2, [V-st in next V-st sp, ch 2, shell in next shell sp, ch 2] around, join with sl st in 3rd ch of beg ch-5.

Rnd 6: (Sl st, beg V-st) in first V-st sp, ch *2, 7 dc in next shell sp, ch 2**, V-st in next V-st sp, rep from * around, ending last rep at **, join with sl st in 3rd ch of beg ch-5.

Rnd 7: (Sl st, beg V-st) in first V-st sp, *ch 2, dc in first dc of 7-dc group, [ch 1, dc in next dc] 6 times, ch 2**, V-st in next V-st sp, rep from * around, ending last rep at **, join with sl st in 3rd ch of beg ch-5.

Rnd 8: (Sl st, beg V-st) in first V-st sp, *ch 2, sc in next ch-1 sp, [ch 3, sc in next ch-1 sp] 5 times, ch 2**, V-st in next V-st sp, rep from * around, ending last rep at **, join with sl st in 3rd ch of beg ch-5.

Rnd 9: (Sl st, beg V-st) in first V-st sp, * ch 3, [sc in next ch-3 sp, ch 3] 5 times**, V-st in next V-st sp, rep from * around, ending last rep at **, join with sl st in 3rd ch of beg ch-5.

Rnd 10: (Sl st, beg V-st, ch 2, dc) in first V-st sp, *ch 3, sk next ch-3 sp, [sc in next ch-3 sp, ch 3] 4 times**, (V-st, ch 2, dc) in next V-st sp, rep from * around, ending last rep at **, join with sl st in 3rd ch of beg ch-5.

Rnd 11: (Sl st, beg V-st) in first V-st sp, *ch 2, V-st in next ch-2 sp, ch 3, sk next ch-3 sp, [sc in next ch-3 sp, ch 3] 3 times**, V-st in next ch-2 sp, rep from * around, ending last rep at **, join with sl st in 3rd ch of beg ch-5.

Rnd 12: (Sl st, beg V-st) in first V-st sp, *ch 2, V-st in next ch-2 sp, ch 2, V-st in next V-st sp, ch 4, sk next ch-3 sp, sc in next ch-3 sp, ch 3, sc in next ch-3 sp, ch 4**, V-st in next V-st sp, rep from * around, ending last rep at **, join with sl st in 3rd ch of beg ch-5. Fasten off.

Rnd 13: With C [E] hook, join CC with a sl st in first V-st sp, beg V-st in same sp, *ch 2, shell in next V-st sp, ch 2, V-st in next V-st sp, ch 4, sc in next ch-3 sp, ch 4**, V-st in next V-st sp, rep from * around, ending last rep at **, join with sl st in 3rd ch of beg ch-2.

Rnd 14: (Sl st, beg V-st) in first V-st sp, *ch 3, 5 dc in next shell sp, ch 3, V-st in next V-st sp, ch 4, sc in next sc, ch 4**, V-st in next V-st sp, rep from * around, ending last rep at **, join with sl st in 3rd ch of beg ch-5.

Rnd 15: (Sl st, beg V-st) in first V-st sp, *ch 4, dc in first dc of 5-dc group, [ch 1, dc in next dc] 4 times, ch 4**, V-st in each of next 2 V-st sps, rep from * around, ending last rep at **, V-st in next V-st sp, join with sl st in 3rd ch of beg ch-5.

Rnd 16: (Sl st, ch 1, sc) in first V-st sp, ch 4, [sc in next sp, ch 4] around, join with sl st in beg sc.

Rnd 17: (Sl st, ch 1, sc) in first sp, ch 5, [sc in next sp, ch 5] around, join with sl st in beg sc. Fasten off.

Sleeve
Make 2.
Rnd 1: With RS facing, using size B [D] hook, join CC with a sl st in rem lp at base of shell in center st of ch-5 at either underarm, ch 1, sc in same st, 2 sc over end sp of next row, 3 sc over end sp of each of next 2 rows, 2 sc over end st of next row, sc in first unworked sp on rnd 7 of Yoke, [sc in next dc, sc in next sp] 13 times, 2 sc over end st of next row, 3 sc over end sp of each of next 2 rows, 2 sc over end sp of next row, join with sl st in beg sc. Turn. *(48 sc)*

Rnd 2: Ch 1, sc in same sc as joining, [ch 4, sk 2 sc, sc in next sc] 3 times, [ch 4, sk next sc, sc in next sc] 15 times, ch 4, [sk 2 sc, sc in next sc, ch 4] twice, join with sl st in beg sc, turn. *(21 sps)*

Row 3: Ch 1, sc in first sp, ch 4, [sc in next sp, ch 4] across, ending with sc in last sp, turn. *(20 sps)*

Rnds 4–10: Rep row 3. At end of rnd 10, do not fasten off. Turn. *(13 sps at end of rnd 10)*

Rnd 11: Ch 1, sc in each of next 13 sps, sc over end st of each of next 8 rows to bottom of armhole, sc over end st of each of next 8 rows, join with sl st in first sc. Do not turn. *(29 sc)*

Rnds 12 & 13: Ch 1, sc in same sc as joining, sc in each rem sc around, join with sl st in first sc. At end of rnd 13, fasten off.

Neckline Trim
With RS facing, using size B [D] hook, join CC with a sl st at corner of left back neck opening, ch 1, sc in same st; working in rem lps of foundation ch across, 5 dc in next st, [sk 2 sts, sc in next st, sk 2 sts, 5 dc in next st] across, sc in same st as last dc made. Fasten off.

Finishing
Beg at center front, weave 1 length of ribbon through ch-1 sps of rnd 7 of Yoke to underarm, weave through sps under Sleeve to back, weave through ch-1 sps of rnd 7 of Yoke to back opening. Rep with length of ribbon on opposite side. Tie a bow in front and in back.

With sewing needle and sewing thread, sew 3 satin roses down center front of Yoke.

BOOTIE
Make 2.
Sole
Rnd 1: Beg at heel, with size B [D] hook and MC. Ch 18, *dc in 4th ch,* dc in 4th ch from hook, 2 dc in next ch, dc in each of next 12 ch, 5 dc in last ch; working in rem lps across opposite side of foundation ch, dc in each of next 12 ch, 2 dc in next ch, join with sl st in last ch of ch-18. *(35 dc)*

Rnd 2: Ch 2 *(counts as first hdc throughout),* 2 hdc in each of next 3 dc, hdc in each of next 11 dc, 2 hdc in each of next 6 dc, hdc in each of next 11 dc, 2 hdc in each of next 3 dc, join with sl st in 2nd ch of beg ch-2. *(47 hdc)*

Rnd 3: Ch 2, [2 hdc in next hdc, hdc in next hdc] 3 times, hdc in each of next 11 hdc, [2 hdc in next st, hdc in next st] 6 times, hdc in each of next 11 hdc, [2 hdc in next hdc, hdc in next hdc] 3 times, join with sl st in 2nd ch of beg ch-2. *(59 hdc)*

Body
Rnd 1: Ch 1; beg in same st as joining, **bpsc** *(see Special Stitches)* over each hdc around, join with sl st in beg bpsc.

Rnds 2–4: Ch 1; sc in same st as joining, sc in each rem sc around, join with sl st in beg sc. At end of rnd 4, fasten off.

Instep
Row 1: Fold Bootie in half to find center st at toe end; with WS facing, count 4 sts to the right of center st; using size B [D] hook, join MC with a sl st in **front lp** *(see Stitch Guide)* only of next st, ch 1, sc in same st; working in front lps only this row, sc in each of next 9 sts, turn. *(10 sc)*

Rows 2–9: Ch 1, sc in each sc across, turn. At end of row 9, do not fasten off.

Join Instep to Body
Mark 10th unworked st on each side of rnd 4 of Body from first and last sts of row 1 of Instep. Working through both thicknesses at once and easing to fit, sc in each of next 10 sts, sc in each rem lp across toe at base of row 1 of Instep; working through both thicknesses at once and easing to fit, sc in each of next 10 sts. Do not fasten off. Do not turn.

Bootie Top
Rnd 1: Ch 4 *(counts as first dc, ch-1;*

working across top of Instep, sk first st, dc in next st, [ch 1, sk next st, dc in next st] 4 times; working around rem unworked sts of rnd 4 of Body, ch 1, sk first st, [dc in next st, ch 1, sk next st] around, join with sl st in 3rd ch of beg ch-4, turn. *(20 ch-1 sps)*

Row 2: Ch 1, sc in same st as joining, [(ch 4, sc) twice in next sp, ch 4, sc in next dc] 15 times, leave rem 5 sps unworked, turn.

Rows 3 & 4: Ch 1, sc in first sp, [ch 4, sc in next sp] across, turn. At end of row 4, fasten off.

Finishing

With sewing needle and sewing thread, tack 1 satin rose at center of row 9 of Instep on each Bootie. Beg at center front, weave ribbon through sps of rnd 1 of Bootie top. Tie in bow at center front. ❏❏

Yellow Rose

SKILL LEVEL

INTERMEDIATE

FINISHED SIZES

Fits 17-inch chest *(6 months)* [18-inch chest *(12 months)*]
Pattern is written for smaller size with changes for larger size in brackets. When only 1 number is given, it applies to both sizes.

FINISHED MEASUREMENT

Chest: 18 [19] inches

MATERIALS

❏ Bernat Softee Baby fine (sport) weight yarn (5 oz/455 yds/140g per skein):
   2 skeins
❏ Sizes B/1/2.25mm [D/3/3.25mm] and C/2/2.75mm [E/4/3.5mm] crochet hooks or sizes needed to obtain gauge
❏ Sewing needle
❏ 2 yds ⅞-inch-wide ribbon
❏ 5 flowers with leaves, ¾-inch
❏ Hook-and-loop fastener
❏ White sewing thread

GAUGE

Size B hook: 10 hdc = 2 inches
Size D hook: 9 hdc = 2 inches

SPECIAL STITCHES

3-double crochet bobble (3-dc bobble): Holding back on hook last lp of each st, work 3 dc in indicated st or sp, yo, draw through all 4 lps on hook.

4-double crochet bobble (4-dc bobble): Holding back on hook last lp of each st, work 4 dc in indicated st or sp, yo, draw through all 5 lps on hook.

5-double crochet bobble (5-dc bobble): Holding back on hook last lp of each st, work 5 dc in indicated st or sp, yo, draw through all 6 lps on hook.

Beginning 4-double crochet bobble (beg 4-dc bobble): (Ch 2; holding back on hook last lp of each st, work 3 dc in indicated st or sp, yo, draw through all 4 lps on hook.

Beginning 5-double crochet bobble (beg 5-dc bobble): (Ch 2; holding back on hook last lp of each st, work 4 dc in indicated st or sp, yo, draw through all 5 lps on hook.

Cluster (cl): Holding back on hook last lp, dc in each of next 6 indicated dc, yo, draw through all 7 lps on hook, ch 1 tightly to secure.

Picot: Ch 4, sc in 4th ch from hook.

Back post single crochet (bpsc): Insert hook from back to front to back around **post** *(see Stitch Guide)* of indicated st, yo, draw up a lp, complete sc.

INSTRUCTIONS

DRESS
Yoke
Row 1: Beg at neck with size B [D] hook, ch 59, sc in 2nd ch from hook, sc in each of next 8 ch, 3 sc in next ch *(corner made),* sc in each of next 9 ch, 3 sc in next ch *(corner made),* sc in each of next 18 ch, [3 sc in next ch *(corner made),* sc in each of next 9 ch] twice, turn. *(66 sc)*

Row 2: Ch 2 *(counts as first hdc throughout),* hdc in each sc across, working 3 hdc in center sc of each 3-sc corner group, turn. *(74 hdc)*

Rows 3–9: Rep row 2. *(130 hdc at end of row 9)*

Row 10: Ch 2, hdc in each of next 18 sts, *ch 8 for armhole, sk next 27 sts*, hdc in each of next 38 sts, rep from * to *, hdc in each of last 19 sts, turn. *(76 hdc)*

Rnd 11: Ch 2, hdc in each rem hdc and in each ch around, join with sl st in 2nd ch of beg ch-2. Do not fasten off. *(92 hdc)*

Skirt
Rnd 1 (RS): With size C [E] hook, ch 5 *(counts as first tr, ch-1),* sk next hdc, [tr in each of next 2 hdc, ch 1, sk next hdc] around, join with sl st in 4th ch of beg ch-5. *(31 ch-1 sps)*

Rnd 2: Ch 1, sc in same st as joining, ch 4, sk next st, [sc in next st, ch 4, sk next st] around, join with sl st in first sc. *(46 ch-4 sps)*

Rnd 3: (Sl st, **beg 4-dc bobble** {*see Special Stitches*}) in first sp, *ch 3, sc in next sp, ch 3**, **4-dc bobble** *(see Special Stitches)* in next sp, rep from * around, ending last rep at **, join with sl st in top of beg 4-dc bobble.

Rnd 4: Ch 1, sc in same st as joining, *ch 3, 4-dc bobble in next sc, ch 3**, sc in next 4-dc bobble, rep from * around, ending last rep at **, join with sl st in beg sc.

Rnd 5: Beg 4-dc bobble in same st as joining, *ch 3, sc in next 4-dc bobble, ch 3**, 4-dc bobble in next sc, rep from * around, ending last rep at **, join with sl st in beg 4-dc bobble.

Rnd 6: Rep rnd 4.

Rnds 7 & 8: Rep rnds 5 and 6, replacing each ch-3 with a ch-4.

Rnds 9 & 10: Rep rnds 5 and 6, replacing each ch-3 with a ch-5.

Rnd 11: Rep 9.

Rnd 12: Ch 1, sc in same st as joining, *ch 6, **5-dc bobble** *(see Special Stitches)* in next sc, ch 6**, sc in next 4-dc bobble, rep from * around, ending last rep at **, join with sl st in beg sc.

Rnd 13: Beg 5-dc bobble *(see Special Stitches)* in same st as joining, *ch 6, sc in next 5-dc bobble, ch 6**, 5-dc bobble in next sc, rep from * around, ending last rep at **, join with sl st in first 4-dc bobble.

Rnd 14: Ch 1, sc in same st as joining, *ch 5, 6 dc in next sc, ch 5**, sc in next 5-dc bobble, rep from * around, ending last rep at **, join with sl st in beg sc.

Rnd 15: Beg 5-dc bobble in same st as joining, *ch 4, dc in each dc of next 6-dc group, ch 4**, 5-dc bobble in next sc, rep from * around, ending last rep at **, join with sl st in beg 5-dc bobble.

Rnd 16: Ch 1, sc in same st as joining, *ch 4, sc over ch sps of last 2 rows tog, ch 5, **cl** *(see Special Stitches)* over 6 dc of next 6-dc group, ch 5, sc over ch sps of last 2 rows tog, ch 4**, sc in top of next 5-dc bobble, rep from * around, ending last rep at **, join with sl st in beg sc.

Rnd 17: (Sl st, ch 1, sc) in first sp, [ch 6, sc in next sp] around, ending with ch 3, dc in first sc to form last ch-6 sp.

Rnds 18 & 19: Ch 1, sc in sp just formed, [ch 6, sc in next sp] around, ending with ch 3, dc in first sc to form last ch-6 sp.

Rnd 20: Ch 1, sc in sp just formed, *ch 4, ({**3-dc bobble** *[see Special Stitches]*, **picot** *[see Special Stitches]*} 3 times, 3-dc bobble) in next sp, ch 4**, sc in next sp, rep from * around, ending last rep at **, join with sl st in beg sc. Fasten off.

Neck Trim
With RS facing, working across rem lps of foundation ch at neck edge of Yoke, join yarn with a sl st in beg st, ch 1, sc in same st, ch 3, sk 2 sts,* 3-dc bobble in next st, ch 3, sk next st, sc in next st**, ch 3, rep from * across to opposite neck corner, ending last rep at **, sl st evenly spaced down back opening to row 1 of Skirt, sl st evenly spaced up opposite side to neck corner, join with sl st in beg sc. Fasten off.

Sleeve
Make 2.
Rnd 1: With size B [D] hook, join yarn with a sl st in 5th ch from the right on ch-8 at bottom of either armhole, ch 1, sc in same st, ch 4, sk next ch, sc in next ch, ch 4, sk next ch, sc in first sk hdc on row 9 of Yoke, ch 4, sc in next hdc, [(ch 4, sk next hdc, sc in next hdc) twice, ch 4, sc in next hdc] 5 times, [ch 4, sk next ch, sc in next ch] twice, ch 2, hdc in first sc to form last ch-4 sp. *(21 ch-4 sps)*

Rnds 2–8: Ch 1, sc in sp just formed, [ch 4, sc in next sp] around, ending with ch 2, hdc in first sc to form last ch-4 sp. At end of rnd 8, do not fasten off.

Cuff
Rnd 1: Ch 1, sc in sp just formed, sc in each sp around, join with sl st in first sc. *(21 sc)*

Rnds 2–4: Ch 1, sc in same sc as

joining, sc in each rem sc around, join with sl st in beg sc. At end of rnd 4, fasten off.

Rep on rem armhole.

Finishing
Beg at center front, weave length of ⅞-inch-wide ribbon through sps of rnd 1 of Skirt. Tie in bow at front.

With sewing needle and thread, sew hook-and-loop fastener at back opening of dress; using photo as a guide, sew 3 flowers with leaves to bottom right corner of Yoke.

BOOTIE
Make 2.
Sole
Rnd 1: With size B [D] hook, beg at heel. Ch 18, dc in 4th ch from hook, 2 dc in next ch, dc in each of next 12 chs, 5 dc in last ch for toe; working in rem lps across opposite side of foundation ch, dc in each of next 12 chs, 2 dc in next ch, join with sl st in last ch of ch-18. *(35 dc)*

Rnd 2: Ch 2 *(counts as first hdc throughout)*, 2 hdc in each of next 3 dc, hdc in each of next 11 dc, 2 hdc in each of next 6 dc, hdc in each of next 11 dc, 2 hdc in each of next 3 dc, join with sl st in 2nd ch of beg ch-2. *(47 hdc)*

Rnd 3: Ch 2, [2 hdc in next hdc, hdc in next hdc] 3 times, hdc in each of next 11 hdc, [2 hdc in next hdc, hdc in next hdc] 6 times, hdc in each of next 11 hdc, [2 hdc in next hdc, hdc in next hdc] 3 times, join with sl st in 2nd ch of beg ch-2. *(59 hdc)*

Sides
Rnd 1: Ch 1, **bpsc** *(see Special Stitches)* over each hdc around, join with sl st in front lp only of first bpsc. Turn.

Rnds 2–4: Ch 1, sc in same st as joining, sc in each rem sc around, join with sl st in first sc, turn. At end of rnd 4, fasten off.

Instep
Row 1: With RS facing, counting joining sc at end of last rnd of Sides as first st, count 25 sc to the left of heel, join CC with sl st in back lp only of next sc, ch 1,

sc in same sc, sc in back lp only of each of next 9 sc across toe, turn. *(10 sc)*

Rows 2–9: Ch 1, sc in each sc across, turn. Do not fasten off at end of row 9.

Connect Instep to Bootie
With heel of Bootie facing, counting joining sc at end of last rnd of Sides as first st, count 16 sts to left of heel and place marker in 16th st; count 16 sts to right of heel and place 2nd marker in 16th st.

With lp still on hook, insert hook in marked st on same side of Bootie where last row of instep ended, complete sc; working towards toe through both thicknesses of Instep and Sides at the same time, sc in each rem lp across base of Instep; working through both thicknesses, sc up opposite side of Instep, ending in rem marked st. Do not fasten off.

Top
Rnd 1: Ch 4 *(counts as first dc, ch-1)*; working toward heel, dc in first unworked sc, ch 1, [sk next unworked sc, dc in next unworked sc, ch 1] 14 times; working across 10 sts at top of Instep, dc in first sc, ch 1, [sk next sc, dc in next sc, ch 1] 4 times, join with sl st in 4th ch of beg ch-4. Do not turn. *(21 ch-1 sps)*

Row 2: Ch 1, sc in same st as joining, *ch 4, [sc, ch 4] 3 times in next sp, sc in next dc, rep from * across to corresponding st on opposite side of instep. Do not work across top of Instep. Turn.

Rows 3 & 4: Sl st in first sp, ch 1, sc in same sp, [ch 4, sc in next sp] across to last sp. Turn. At end of row 4, fasten off.

Finishing
Beg at center front, weave 1 length of ⅞-inch-wide ribbon through sps on rnd 1 of Bootie Top on each Bootie. Tie in bow at front.

With sewing needle and thread, sew 1 flower with leaves at center of Instep on each Bootie. ❏

SKILL LEVEL

INTERMEDIATE

FINISHED SIZE

Fits 17-inch chest *(3–6 months)*

FINISHED MEASUREMENT

Chest: 19 inches

MATERIALS

❑ Size 10 crochet cotton:
   1200 yds white
❑ Size 0/2.5mm steel crochet hook
   or size needed to obtain gauge
❑ Sewing needle
❑ 3 yds ¼-inch-wide pink ribbon
❑ White sewing thread

GAUGE

16 sc = 3 inches with 2 strands
held tog

PATTERN NOTE

Work with 2 strands held together
as 1 throughout.

SPECIAL STITCHES

Long double crochet (ldc): Yo,
insert hook in indicated st, yo, draw
up a lp to ½ inch, [yo, pull through
2 lps on hook] twice.

**Wrapped double crochet group
(wdcg):** Dc in each of next 3 sts;
working horizontally over **posts**
(see Stitch Guide) of all 3 sts tog, 2
dc over last 3 dc made.

**Beginning wrapped double
crochet group (beg wdcg):** Ch
3, dc in same st as ch-3, dc in each
of next 2 sts; working horizontally
over posts of all 3 sts tog, 2 dc over
last 3 dc made.

**Ending wrapped double crochet
group (end wdcg):** Wdcg over
last 3 sts, dc in same st as last dc of
3-dc group.

INSTRUCTIONS

SWEATER

Yoke

Row 1: Beg at neck, ch 80, dc in 4th
ch from hook, dc in each of next 11
ch, 5 dc in next ch *(corner made)*, dc

in each of next 14 ch, 5 dc in next
ch *(corner made)*, dc in each of next
20 ch, 5 dc in next ch, dc in each
of next 14 ch, 5 dc in next ch, dc in
each of next 13 ch, turn. *(94 dc)*
Note: *Remainder of yoke is worked in
back lps (see Stitch Guide) only.*
Row 2: Ch 1, sc in each dc across,
working 3 sc in center dc at each
corner, turn. *(102 sc)*
Rows 3 & 4: Ch 1, sc in each sc
across, working 3 sc in center sc at
each corner, turn. *(118 sc at end of
row 4)*
Row 5: Ch 3 *(counts as first ldc)*, **ldc**
(see Special Stitches) in each rem sc
across, working 5 ldc in center sc of
each corner. *(134 ldc)*
Rows 6–12: Rep rows 2–5 alternately,
ending with row 4. Do not fasten off
at end of row 12. Turn. *(198 sc at
end of row 12)*

Body

Note: *Body is worked in both lps unless
otherwise stated.*
Row 1 (RS): Beg wdcg *(see Special
Stitches)*, sc in next sc, *[ch 2, **wdcg**
(see Special Stitches), sc in next st]*
across to first sc of next 3-sc group,
**insert hook in center sc of 3-sc
group; skipping sc sts between same
3-sc group and next 3-sc group for
armhole, insert hook in center sc
of next 3-sc group, yo, draw up a
lp, yo, draw through both lps on
hook**, sc in next sc, work from
* to * 12 times, sk first sc of 3-sc
group, work from ** to **, sc in next
sc, work from * to * 6 times, ch 2,
end wdcg *(see Special Stitches)*,
turn. *(26 wdcg)*
Row 2: Ch 1, *sk top of first dc in next
2-dc horizontal group, sc in top of
next horizontal dc, ch 2, wdcg over
next 3 dc**, ch 2, rep from * across
to last wdcg, ending last rep at **,
dc in top of turning ch, turn.
Row 3: Ch 1, *sk top of first dc in next
2-dc horizontal group, sc in top of
next horizontal dc, ch 2, wdcg over
next 3 dc**, ch 2, rep from * across
to last wdcg, ending last rep at **,
dc in last sc, turn.

Rep row 3 until Body measures 6½
inches from beg or desired length,
ending with a RS row. Fasten off.

Neck Edging

With RS facing, working in rem lps
across foundation ch at base of Yoke,
attach thread with a sl st in first rem
lp, [ch 3, sk next st, sl st in next st]
across. Fasten off.

Sleeve
Make 2.

Rnd 1: With RS facing, join thread
with a sl st over side of joining st at
either armhole opening; working in
sk sc of row 12 of Yoke, ch 2, sk first
sk sc, *wdcg over next 3 sc, ch 2, sc
in next sc, ch 2, sk next sc, rep from
* around, ending with wdcg over last
3 dc, ch 2, sl st at base of beg ch-2,
turn. *(9 wdcg)*
Rnd 2: Ch 1, sl st in each of next 2 chs
and in top of next horizontal dc, sc in
next horizontal dc, *ch 2, wdcg over
next 3 dc, ch 2**, sk next horizontal
dc, sc in top of next horizontal dc,
rep from * around, ending last rep
at **, sl st in first sc, turn.
Rep rnd 2 until Sleeve measures 6
inches or desired length, ending
with a WS rnd. Do not fasten off at
end of last rnd. Turn.

Cuff

Rnd 1 (RS): Ch 1, sl st in each st across
to first dc of first wdcg, ch 1, 2 sc
in same dc, sc in center dc of same
wdcg, sc in next dc, sc in each of 3
dc of each wdcg around, join with
sl st in **front lp** *(see Stitch Guide)*
only of first sc, turn. *(28 sc)*
Rnd 2: Ch 1; beg in same sc as joining,
sc in **back lp** *(see Stitch Guide)* only
of each rem sc around, join with sl st
in front lp only of beg sc, turn.
Rnds 3 & 4: Rep rnd 2. At end of rnd
4, join with sl st in both lps of beg
sc, turn.
Rnd 5: [Ch 3, sk next st, sl st in next
st] around, join with sl st at base of
beg ch-3. Fasten off. *(14 ch-3 sps)*
Rep on rem armhole opening.

Finishing

Cut 4 lengths of ribbon each 10 inches long. With sewing needle and white sewing thread, tack end of 1 length to end st of first row on RS of Left Yoke. Tack 2nd length to end st of last row on RS side of Left Yoke. Tack rem lengths to end sts on RS of Right Yoke opposite first 2 lengths.

BONNET
Back

Row 1: Ch 23, sc in 2nd ch from hook, sc in each of next 20 ch, 5 sc in last ch; working in rem lps across opposite side of foundation ch, sc in each of next 21 ch, turn. *(47 sc)*

Note: *Remainder of Back is worked in back lps only.*

Row 2: Ch 1, sc in each of first 3 sc, ldc in each of next 19 sc, 5 ldc in next sc *(corner made)*, ldc in next sc, 5 ldc in next sc *(corner made)*, ldc in each of next 19 sc, sc in each of next 3 sc, turn. *(55 sts)*

Row 3: Ch 1, sc in each st across, working 3 sc in center st of each corner group, turn. *(59 sc)*

Rows 4 & 5: Rep row 3. *(67 sc at end of row 5)*

Row 6: Ch 1, sc in each of first 3 sc, ldc in each sc across to center sc of first corner, 5 ldc in center sc, ldc in each sc across to center st of next corner, 5 ldc in center sc, ldc in each rem sc across to last 3 sc, sc in each of last 3 sc, turn. *(75 sts)*

Rows 7–9: Rep row 3. *(87 sc at end of row 9)*

Row 10: Rep row 6. *(95 sts)*

Rows 11 & 12: Rep row 3. *(103 sc at end of row 12)*

Row 13: Ch 1, sc in each sc across, working 2 sc in center sc of each corner group, turn. Do not fasten off. *(105 sc)*

Front

Note: *Front is worked in both lps unless otherwise stated.*

Row 1: Ch 1, sc in first sc, ch 2, *sk 2 sc, wdcg over next 3 sc, sk 2 sc**, sc in next sc, ch 2, rep from * across, ending last rep at **, dc in last sc, turn. *(13 wdcg)*

Row 2: Ch 1, *sk top of first dc in next 2-dc horizontal group, sc in top of next horizontal dc, ch 2, wdcg over next 3 dc**, rep from * across to last wdcg, ending last rep at **, dc in last sc, turn.

Rows 3–11: Rep row 2. At end of row 11, fasten off.

Brim & Neck Edging

Note: *Fold last 3 rows back over RS to form Brim.*

Row 1: With RS facing, working through both thicknesses of Brim and Bonnet Front below, join thread with sl st at corner, ch 1, sc in same st, sc across edge of Brim; working over ends of rows of Front, sc evenly spaced across to bottom of Back, skipping sts as necessary to slightly gather bottom, sc across ends of rows across opposite Front, working through both thicknesses where Brim is folded back, turn.

Rows 2–4: Ch 1; working in back lps only, sc in each sc across, turn. At end of row 4, fasten off.

Finishing

Cut a 28-inch length of ribbon. Weave through sps on last row of Bonnet Brim.

BOOTIE
Make 2.
Sole

Rnd 1: Beg at heel, ch 18, *dc in 4th ch,* dc in 4th ch from hook, 2 dc in next ch, dc in each of next 12 chs, 5 dc in last ch for toe; working in rem lps across opposite side of foundation ch, dc in each of next 12 chs, 2 dc in next ch, join with sl st in last ch of ch-18. *(35 dc)*

Rnd 2: Ch 2 *(counts as first hdc throughout)*, 2 hdc in each of next 3 dc, hdc in each of next 11 dc, 2 hdc in each of next 6 dc, hdc in each of next 11 dc, 2 hdc in each of next 3 dc, join with sl st in 2nd ch of beg ch-2. *(47 hdc)*

Rnd 3: Ch 2, [2 hdc in next hdc, hdc in next hdc] 3 times, hdc in each of next 11 hdc, [2 hdc in next hdc, hdc in next hdc] 6 times, hdc in each of next 11 hdc, [2 hdc in next hdc, hdc in next hdc] 3 times, join with sl st in 2nd ch of beg ch-2. *(59 hdc)*

Sides

Rnd 1: Ch 1, **bpsc** *(see Special Stitches)* over each hdc around, join with sl st in front lp only of beg bpsc, turn.

Rnd 2: Ch 1; beg in same st as joining, working in back lps only this rnd, sc in each sc around, join with sl st in beg sc, turn.

Rnd 3: Ch 3 *(counts as first dc throughout)*, ldc in each sc around, join with sl st in 3rd ch of beg ch-3, turn.

Rnd 4: Ch 1, sc in same st as joining, sc in each rem ldc around, join with sl st in top of first sc, turn.

Rnds 5 & 6: Ch 1; working in back lps only, sc in each sc around, join with sl st in beg sc. At end of rnd 6, fasten off.

Instep

Row 1: With heel of Bootie facing, counting joining sc at end of last rnd of Sides as first st, count 25 sc to the left of heel, join thread with sl st in back lp only of next sc, ch 1, sc in same sc, sc in back lp only of each of next 9 sc, turn. *(10 sc)*

Row 2: Ch 1, sc in each sc across, turn.

Row 3: Ch 3, ldc in each rem sc across, turn.

Rows 4–7: Ch 1; working in back lps only, sc in each st across, turn. At end of row 7, do not fasten off.

Connect Instep to Bootie

With heel of Bootie facing, counting joining sc at end of last rnd of Sides as first st, count 16 sts to left of heel and place marker in 16th st; count 16 sts to right of heel and place 2nd marker in 16th st.

With lp still on hook, insert hook in marked st on same side of Bootie where last row of Instep ended, complete sc; working towards toe through both thicknesses of Instep and Sides at the same time, sc evenly spaced down Instep to toe, sc in each rem lp across base of Instep; working through both thicknesses, sc up opposite side of Instep, ending in rem marked st. Do not fasten off. Do not turn.

Top

Rnd 1: Ch 4 *(counts as first dc, ch-1)*; working toward heel, dc in first unworked sc, ch 1, [sk next unworked sc, dc in next unworked sc, ch 1] 14 times; working across 10 sts at top

of Instep, dc in first sc, ch 1, [sk next sc, dc in next sc, ch 1] 4 times, join with sl st in 4th ch of beg ch-4. Do not turn. (21 ch-1 sps)

Rnd 2: Ch 1, sc in same dc as joining, sc in next sp, [sc in next dc, sc in next sp] 6 times, [**sc dec** (*see Stitch Guide*) over next dc and next sp] twice, [sc in next dc, sc in next sp] around, join with sl st in beg sc. Do

not turn. (40 sts)

Rnd 3: Ch 2, sk next st, [wdcg, sc in next st, ch 2, sk next st] around, ending with wdcg, sl st at base of first ch-2. Turn. (8 wdcg)

Rnd 4: Ch 1, sl st in top of last horizontal dc made, sc in top of next horizontal dc, *ch 2, wdcg over next 3 dc**, sk next horizontal dc, sc in top of next horizontal dc, rep from * around,

ending last rep at **, join with sl st in beg sc. Turn.

Rnd 5: Rep rnd 4. Fasten off.

Finishing
Cut 2 lengths of ribbon each 14 inches long. Weave 1 length through ch-1 sps on rnd 1 of Top on each Bootie. ❏❏

Lily of the Valley

SKILL LEVEL

INTERMEDIATE

FINISHED SIZES
Fits 18-inch chest (*6 months*) [20-inch chest (*12 months*)]
Pattern is written for smaller size with changes for larger size in brackets. When only 1 number is given, it applies to both sizes.

FINISHED MEASUREMENT
Chest: 20 [22] inches

MATERIALS
6 months
❏ Red Heart Soft Baby fine (sport) weight yarn (7 oz/594 yds per skein):
   2 skeins #7001 white
❏ Size C/2/2.75mm and D/3/3.25mm crochet hooks or sizes needed to obtain gauge
12 months
❏ Bernat Softee Baby fine (sport) weight yarn (5 oz/455 yds/140g per skein):
   2 skeins #02000 white
❏ Size D/3/3.25mm and E/4/3.5mm crochet hooks or sizes needed to obtain gauge
Both sizes
❏ Sewing needle
❏ 4 yds (¼-inch-wide) satin ribbon
❏ 3 (⅜-inch-diameter) buttons
❏ 7 satin 1¼-inch-diameter roses with leaves
❏ White sewing thread

GAUGE
Size C hook and Red Heart Soft
Baby: 24 dc = 4 inches
Size D hook and Bernat Softee
Baby: 22 dc = 4 inches

SPECIAL STITCHES
Large shell (lg shell): (3 dc, ch 3, 3 dc) in indicated st or sp.
Small shell (sm shell): (2 dc, ch 2, 2 dc) in indicated st or sp.
Beginning small shell (beg sm shell): (Ch 3, dc, ch 2, 2 dc) in indicated st or sp.
Puff stitch (puff st): *Yo, insert hook in indicated st, yo, draw up a lp to approximately ⅜ inch, rep from * twice in same st, yo, draw through all 7 lps on hook, ch 1 tightly to secure.
Beginning puff stitch (beg puff st): Ch 3, [yo, insert hook in st at base of ch-3, yo, draw up a lp to approximately ⅜ inch] twice, yo, draw through all 5 lps on hook, ch 1 tightly to secure.
V-stitch (V-st): (Dc, ch 3, dc) in indicated st or sp.
Picot: Ch 5, sc in 4th ch from hook.

INSTRUCTIONS
DRESS
Yoke
Row 1: Beg at neck, with size C [D] hook, ch 79, sc in 2nd ch from hook, sc in each rem ch across, turn. (78 sc)

Row 2: Ch 3 (*counts as first dc throughout*), dc in each of next 13 sc, 5 dc in next sc (*corner made*), dc in each of next 14 sc, 5 dc in next sc (*corner made*), dc in each of next 18 sc, 5 dc in next sc (*corner made*), dc in each of next 14 sc, 5 dc in next sc (*corner made*), dc in each of last 14 sc, turn. (94 dc)

Row 3: Ch 1, sc in each dc across, working 3 sc in center dc of each corner, turn. (102 sc)

Row 4: Ch 3, dc in each sc across, working 5 dc in center sc of each corner, turn. (118 dc)

Rows 5–10: Rep rows 3 and 4 alternately. (190 dc at end of row 10)

Row 11: Ch 1, sc in each dc across to center dc of first corner, *sc in center dc, ch 8 for armhole, sk next 42 dc, sc in center dc of next corner*, sc in each dc across to center dc of next corner, rep from * to *, sc in each rem dc across, turn. (106 sc, 16 chs)

Row 12: Ch 3, dc in each sc and ch st across, turn. (122 dc)

Row 13: Ch 1, sc in each dc across, turn.

Note: *Do not turn rem rnds unless otherwise stated.*

Rnd 14 (RS): Ch 4 (*counts as first dc, ch-1*), sk next sc, [dc in each of next 2 sc, ch 1, sk next sc] around, join with sl st in 3rd ch of beg ch-4. Do not turn. (41 ch-1 sps, 81 dc)

Rnd 15: Ch 1, sc in same st as joining, [sc in each dc, 2 sc in each ch-1 sp] around, working 3 sc in each of 3 ch-1 sps under each armhole opening, join with sl st in beg sc. (169 sc)

Skirt
Rnd 1: With size D [E] hook, ch 1, sc in same sc as joining, [ch 4, sk next 2 sc, sc in next sc] around, join with sl st in beg sc. (56 ch-3 sps)

Rnd 2: Sl st into first ch-4 sp, ch 1, sc in same sp, ch 4, [sc in next sp, ch 4] around, join with sl st in beg sc.

Rnd 3: Sl st into first ch-4 sp, ch 3, 4 dc in same sp, *ch 1, sc in next sp,

ch 1, **lg shell** (see Special Stitches) in next sp, ch 1, sc in next sp, ch 1**, 5 dc in next sp, rep from * around, ending last rep at **, join with sl st in 3rd ch of beg ch-3. (14 lg shells, 14 5-dc groups)

Rnd 4: Ch 3, *[2 dc in next dc, dc in next dc] twice, ch 2, **sm shell** (see Special Stitches) in next lg shell sp, ch 2**, dc in first dc of next 5-dc group, rep from * around, ending last rep at **, join with sl st in 3rd ch of beg ch-3.

Rnd 5: Beg puff st (see Special Stitches) in same st as joining, *[ch 3, sk next dc, **puff st** (see Special Stitches) in next dc] 3 times, ch 3, dc in next sm shell sp, ch 3**, puff st in first dc of next 7-dc group, rep from * around, ending last rep at **, join with sl st in top of beg puff st.

Rnd 6: Sl st in first ch-3 sp, ch 1, sc in same sp, *ch 3, **V-st** (see Special Stitches) in next sp, ch 3, sc in each of next 2 sps, ch 4**, sc in each of next 2 sps, rep from * around, ending last rep at **, sc in last sp, join with sl st in first sc.

Rnd 7: Sl st in each of next 3 chs, sl st in first dc of V-st, (sl st, ch 3, 4 dc) in V-st sp, *ch 2, sc in next sp, ch 2, lg shell in ch-4 sp, ch 2, sc in next sp, ch 2**, 5 dc in next V-st sp, rep from * around, ending last rep at **, join with sl st in 3rd of beg ch-3.

Rnds 8–37: Rep rnds 4–7 consecutively.

Rnd 38: Sl st in first sp, beg puff st in same sp, [**picot** (see Special Stitches), ch 1, puff st in next sp] twice, *picot, ch 1, sc in each of next 2 sps**, [picot, ch 1, puff st in next sp] 3 times, rep from * around, ending last rep at **, picot, ch 1, join with sl st in top of beg puff st. Fasten off.

Neck & Back Opening Edging

Rnd 1: With RS facing, using size C [D] hook, attach yarn with a sl st at right neck corner, ch 1, sc in same st, sc evenly spaced down right back opening, sc evenly spaced up left back opening to corner, 3 sc in corner st, sc evenly spaced across neck to right neck corner, 2 sc in same st as first sc, join with sl st in beg sc.

Row 2: Ch 1, sc in same st as joining, sc down right back opening, sc evenly spaced up left back opening, working

(ch 3, sc in next sc) 3 times evenly spaced for buttonholes, ending with sc in first sc of 3-sc group at opposite corner. Fasten off.

Sleeve
Make 2.

Rnd 1: With RS facing, using size C [D] hook, working in 42 sk sts on yoke and in rem lps of 8 chs at armhole opening, join yarn with a sl st in st at bottom center of either armhole opening, ch 1, sc in same st, *ch 3, sk 2 sts, sc in next st, ch 3, sk next st**, sc in next st, rep from * around, ending last rep at ** around, join with sl st in beg sc. (20 ch-3 sps)

Rnd 2: (Sl st, ch 3, 4 dc) in first ch-3 sp, *ch 1, sc in next sp, ch 1, sm shell in next sp, ch 1, sc in next sp, ch 1**, 5 dc in next sp, rep from * around, ending last rep at **, join with sl st in 3rd ch of first ch-3.

Rnd 3: Ch 3, *[2 dc in next dc, dc in next dc] twice, ch 2, V-st st in next sm-shell sp, ch 2**, dc in first dc of next 5-dc group, rep from * around, ending last rep at **, join with sl st in 3rd ch of beg ch-3.

Rnd 4: Beg puff st in same st as joining, *[ch 3, sk next dc, puff st in next dc] 3 times, ch 2, dc in next V-st sp, ch 2**, puff st in first dc of next 7-dc group, rep from * around, ending last rep at **, join with sl st in top of beg puff st.

Rnd 5: (Sl st, ch 1, sc) in first sp, *ch 2, V-st in next sp, ch 2, sc in each of next 2 sps, ch 3**, sc in each of next 2 sps, rep from * around, ending last rep at **, sc in next sp, join with sl st in beg sc.

Rnd 6: Sl st in each of next 2 chs and in first dc of V-st, (sl st, ch 3, 4 dc) in same sp, *ch 1, sc in next sp, ch 1, sm shell in next sp, ch 1, sc in next sp, ch 1**, 5 dc in next sp, rep from * around, ending last rep at **, join with sl st in 3rd ch of beg ch-3.

Rnds 7–9: Rep rnds 3–5. At end of rnd 9, do not fasten off.

Cuff

Rnd 1: (Sl st, ch 1, sc) in first ch-2 sp, sc in each of next 2 sps, 2 sc in next ch-3 sp, [sc in each of next 3 sps, 2 sc in next ch-3 sp] around, join with sl st in beg sc. (25 sc)

Rnds 2 & 3: Ch 1, sc in same sc as joining, sc in each rem sc around, join with sl st in beg sc. At end of rnd 3, fasten off.

Finishing

Beg at center front, weave ribbon through ch-1 sps of rnd 14 of Yoke. Tie in bow at front. Cut ends to desired length. Tack 1 satin rose to Yoke just above bow. Tack 1 satin rose to each end of ribbon. Sew buttons on back of dress opposite buttonholes.

BONNET
Crown

Rnd 1: With D [E] hook, ch 6, join to form a ring, ch 1, 12 sc in ring, join with sl st in beg sc. (12 sc)

Rnd 2: Ch 3 (counts as first dc throughout), dc in same sc as joining, 2 dc in each rem sc around, join with sl st in 3rd ch of beg ch-3. (24 dc)

Rnd 3: Ch 3, dc in next dc, 2 dc in next dc, [dc in each of next 2 dc, 2 dc in next dc] around, join with sl st in 3rd ch of beg ch-3. (32 dc)

Rnds 4 & 5: Ch 3, 2 dc in next dc, [dc in next dc, 2 dc in next dc] around, join with sl st in 3rd ch of beg ch-3. (72 dc at end of rnd 5)

Rnd 6: Rep rnd 3. (96 dc)
Do not fasten off.

Front

Row 1 (RS): Ch 1, sc in same dc as joining, [ch 3, sk 2 dc, sc in next dc] 26 times, turn. (26 ch-3 sps)

Row 2: (Sl st, ch 1, sc) in first sp, [ch 3, sc in next sc] across, turn. (25 ch-3 sps)

Row 3: (Sl st, **beg sm shell** (see Special Stitches)) in first sp, *ch 1, sc in next sp, ch 1, 5 dc in next sp, ch 1, sc in next sp, ch 1, sm shell in next sp, rep from * across, turn. (7 sm shells, 6 5-dc groups)

Row 4: Sl st in each of first 2 dc, (sl st, beg sm shell) in next sm-shell sp, *ch 1, dc in first dc of next 5-dc group, [2 dc in next dc, dc in next dc] twice, ch 1**, V-st in next sm-shell sp, rep from * across to last sm shell, ending last rep at **, sm shell in last sm-shell sp, turn.

Row 5: Sl st in each of first 2 dc, (sl st, beg sm shell) in next sm-shell sp, ch 3, *puff st in first dc of next 7-dc group, [3 ch, sk next dc, puff st in next dc] 3 times, ch 2**, dc in next V-st sp, ch 2, rep from * across to last sm shell, ending last rep at **, sm shell in next sm-shell sp, turn.

Row 6: Sl st in each of first 2 dc, (sl st, beg sm shell) in next sm-shell sp, *sc in each of next 2 sps, ch 2, V-st in next sp, ch 2, sc in each of next 2 sps**, ch 3, rep from * across to last sm shell, ending last rep at **, sm shell in last sm-shell sp, turn.

Row 7: Sl st in each of first 2 dc, (sl st, beg sm shell) in next sm-shell sp, *ch 2, sc in next sp, ch 2, 5 dc in V-st sp, ch 2, sc in next sp, ch 2, sm shell in next sp, rep from * across, turn.

Rows 8–13: Rep rows 4–7 consecutively, ending with row 5. At end of row 13, do not fasten off. Do not turn.

Brim & Neck Edging

Row 1: Ch 1; working over ends of rows of Front, sc evenly spaced across to unworked sts at bottom of Crown, sc evenly spaced across bottom of Crown, skipping sts as necessary to slightly gather bottom, sc across ends of rows across opposite Front to end st of last row, turn.

Rows 2 & 3: Ch 1, sc in each sc across, turn. At end of row 3, fasten off.

Finishing

Weave length of ribbon through sps on rnd 12 of Bonnet. Tack 1 satin rose at bottom corner on each side of Front.

BOOTIE
Make 2.

Rnd 1: Beg at heel, with size C [D] hook, ch 16, sc in 2nd ch from hook, sc in each of next 13 ch, 3 sc in last ch for toe; working in rem lps across opposite side of foundation ch, sc in each of next 13 ch, 2 sc in last ch, join with sl st in beg sc. *(32 sc)*

Rnd 2: Ch 1, 2 sc in same sc as joining, sc in each of next 13 sc, 2 sc in each of next 3 sc, sc in each of next 13 sc, 2 sc in each of last 2 sc, join with sl st in beg sc. *(38 sc)*

Rnds 3–6: Ch 1, beg in same sc as joining, sc in each sc around, inc 3 sc evenly spaced at heel and toe on each rnd, join with sl st in beg sc. *(62 sc at end of rnd 6)*

Rnd 7: Ch 1, sc in same sc as joining, sc in each rem sc around, join with sl st in beg sc.

Rnd 8: Ch 1, sc in same sc as joining, sc in each rem sc around, working 2 **sc decs** *(see Stitch Guide)* evenly spaced at toe and at heel, join with sl st in beg sc. *(58 sts)*

Rnd 9: Ch 1, sc in same st as joining, sc in each rem st around, working 4 sc decs evenly spaced at toe, join with sl st in beg sc. *(54 sts)*

Rnd 10: Rep rnd 8. *(50 sts)*

Rnds 11 & 12: Rep rnds 9 and 10. *(42 sts at end of rnd 12)*

Rnd 13: Ch 1; sc in same st as joining, sc in each rem sc around, working 2 sc decs evenly spaced at toe, join with sl st in beg sc. *(40 sts)*

Rnd 14: Ch 4 *(counts as first dc, ch-1)*, [sk next st, dc in next st, ch 1] around, join with sl st in 3rd ch of beg ch-4. *(20 ch-1 sps)*

Rnd 15: Ch 1, sc in same st as joining, *ch 5, (sc, ch 5) 3 times in next sp, sc in next dc, rep from * around, ending with ch 5, ({sc, ch 5} twice, sc) in last sp, ch 2, dc in beg sc to form last ch-5 sp.

Rnd 16: Ch 1, sc in sp just formed, [ch 5, sc in next sp] around, ending with ch 2, dc in beg sc to form last ch-5 sp.

Rnd 17: Ch 1, sc in sp just formed, ch 5, [sc in next sp, ch 5] around, join with sl st in beg sc. Fasten off.

Finishing

Beg at center front, weave length of ribbon through ch-1 sps of rnd 14 on each Bootie. Tie ends in bow and trim to desired length. Tack 1 satin rose to each Bootie front directly beneath bow. ❏❏

SKILL LEVEL

INTERMEDIATE

FINISHED SIZE
Fits 17-inch chest (3–6 months)

FINISHED MEASUREMENT
Chest: 19 inches

MATERIALS
- ❑ Size 10 crochet cotton: 2000 yds white
- ❑ Size 0/2.5mm steel crochet hook or size needed to obtain gauge
- ❑ 4½ yds ⅜-inch-wide pink ribbon

GAUGE
[Dc, ch 1] 3 times = 1 inch with 2 strands held tog

PATTERN NOTE
Work with 2 strands held together as 1 throughout.

SPECIAL STITCHES
Shell: ({Dc, ch 1} twice, dc) in indicated st or sp.

V-stitch (V-st): (Dc, ch 1, dc) in indicated st or sp.

Beginning V-stitch (beg V-st): (Ch 4, dc) in indicated st or sp.

INSTRUCTIONS
SWEATER
Yoke
Row 1 (RS): Beg at neck, ch 76, dc in 6th ch from hook, [ch 1, sk next ch, dc in next ch] 4 times, *ch 1, sk next ch, (dc, ch 1) 5 times in next ch (corner made), sk next ch, dc in next ch*, [ch 1, sk next ch, dc in next ch] 5 times, rep from * to *, [ch 1, sk next ch, dc in next ch] 8 times, rep from * to *, [ch 1, sk next ch, dc in next ch] 5 times, rep from * to *, [ch 1, sk next ch, dc in next ch] across, turn. (52 ch-1 sps)

Row 2: Ch 1, sc in first dc, [tr in next sp, pushing "bump" to RS, sc in next dc] across, ending with tr in turning ch-4 sp, sc in 3rd ch of turning ch-4, turn. (52 tr)

Row 3: Ch 4 (counts as first dc, ch-1 throughout), [dc in next sc, ch 1] across, working (dc, ch 1) 3 times in sc at center of each corner, ending with dc in last sc, turn. (60 ch-1 sps)

Rows 4–10: Rep rows 2 and 3 alternately, ending with row 2. (84 tr at end of row 10) Do not fasten off. Remove hook from lp.

With 2 strands held tog, attach new piece of thread over center sc of first corner, ch 1, sc in same sc, ch 6, sc in center sc of next corner for first armhole. Rep on rem 2 corners for 2nd armhole.

Body
Row 1: Pick up dropped lp, ch 3 (counts as first dc), [sk next tr, dc in next sc, ch 1, sk next tr, **shell** (see Special Stitches) in next sc, ch 1, sk next tr, dc in next sc] 4 times, sk first ch of ch-6, dc in next ch, ch 1, sk next ch, shell in next ch, ch 1, sk next ch, dc in next ch, [dc in next sc, ch 1, sk next tr, shell in next sc, ch 1, sk next tr, dc in next sc, sk next tr] 7 times, dc in next sc, ch 1, sk next tr, shell in next sc, ch 1, dc in first ch of ch-6, sk next ch, dc in next ch, ch 1, sk next ch, shell in next ch, ch 1, dc in next ch, dc in next sc, [ch 1, sk next tr, shell in next sc, ch 1, sk next tr, dc in next sc, sk next tr, dc in next sc] 4 times, turn. (18 shells)

Row 2: Ch 1, sc in first dc, sc in each rem dc and tr in each rem ch-1 sp across. (72 tr, 92 sc)

Row 3: Ch 3, sk next sc and next tr, *dc in next sc, ch 1, shell in next sc, ch 1, dc in next sc**, sk next tr, next 2 sc and next tr, rep from * across, ending last rep at **, sk next tr and next sc, dc in last sc, turn. (18 shells)

Rows 4–20: Rep rows 2 and 3 alternately, ending with a row 2. Fasten off at end of row 20.

Sleeve
Make 2.
Rnd 1: With RS facing, join thread with a sl st in rem lp of first ch of ch-6 at either underarm, ch 4 (counts as first dc, ch-1), sk next ch, shell in next ch, ch 1, sk next ch, dc in next ch, sk first tr on underarm, *dc in next sc, ch 1, sk next tr, shell in next sc, ch 1, sk next tr, dc in next sc, sk next tr, rep from * around, join with sl st in 3rd ch of beg ch-4, turn. (7 shells)

Rnd 2: Ch 1, sc in same st as joining, sc in each dc and tr in each ch-1 sp around, join with sl st in first sc, turn. (35 sc, 28 tr)

Rnd 3: Sl st in next tr and in next sc, ch 4, *shell in next sc, ch 1, dc in next sc, sk [tr, 2 sc, tr], dc in next sc, ch 1, rep from * around, join with sl st in 3rd ch of beg ch-4, turn. (7 shells)

Rep rnds 2 and 3 alternately until Sleeve measures 6 inches or desired length, ending with rnd 2. Do not fasten off.

Cuff
Rnd 1: With RS facing, ch 3, dc in same st as joining, dc in each rem sc around, join with sl st in 3rd ch of beg ch-3, turn. (36 dc)

Rnd 2: Ch 1, sc in same dc as joining, tr in next dc, [sc in next dc, tr in next dc] around, join with sl st in first sc, turn. (18 tr, 18 sc)

Rnd 3: Ch 4, [dc, in next sc, ch 1] around, join with sl st in 3rd ch of beg ch-4, turn. (18 ch-1 sps)

Rnd 4: Ch 1, sc in same st as joining, tr in next sp, [sc in next dc, tr in next sp] around, join with sl st in beg sc. Fasten off.

Finishing
Cut a 30-inch length of ribbon and weave through rnd 1 of Yoke. Cut a 42-inch length of ribbon and weave through rnd 9 of Yoke. Cut 2 lengths of ribbon each 14 inches long. Weave 1 through rnd 3 of each Cuff.

BONNET
Crown
Rnd 1 (RS): Ch 6, join with sl st to form ring, ch 4, [dc in ring, ch 1] 11 times, join with sl st in 3rd ch of first ch-4, turn. (12 ch-1 sps)

Rnd 2: Ch 1, beg in same st as joining, sc in each dc and tr in each ch-1 sp around, join with sl st in beg sc, turn. (12 sc, 12 tr)

Rnd 3: Ch 4, (dc, ch 1) in each st around, join with sl st in 3rd ch of beg ch-4, turn. *(24 ch-1 sps)*
Rnd 4: Rep rnd 2. *(24 sc, 24 tr)*
Rnd 5: Ch 4, *V-st *(see Special Stitches)* in next sc**, [ch 1, dc in next sc] 3 times, ch 1, rep from * around, ending last rep at **, [ch 1, dc in next sc] twice, ch 1, join with sl st in 3rd ch of beg ch-4, turn. *(30 ch-1 sps)*
Rnd 6: Rep rnd 2. *(30 sc, 30 tr)*
Rnd 7: Beg V-st *(see Special Stitches)* in same st as joining, *[ch 1, dc in next sc] twice, ch 1**, V-st in next sc, rep from * around, ending last rep at **, join with sl st in 3rd ch of beg ch-4, turn. *(40 ch-1 sps)*
Rnd 8: Rep rnd 2. *(40 sc, 40 tr)*

Brim
Row 1 (RS): Ch 3, [dc in next sc, ch 1, shell in next sc, ch 1, dc in next sc] 11 times, dc in next sc, leave rem 11 sts unworked, turn. *(11 shells)*
Row 2: Ch 1, sc in each dc and tr in each ch-1 sp across, ending with sc in last dc, sc in top of turning ch-3, turn. *(44 tr, 57 sc)*
Row 3: Ch 3, sk next sc, *dc in next sc, ch 1, shell in next sc, ch 1, dc in next sc**, sk (next tr, next 2 sc, next tr), rep from * across, ending last rep at **, sk next tr and next sc, dc in last sc, turn. *(11 shells)*
Row 4: Rep row 2.
Rows 5–14: Rep rows 3 and 4 alternately. Do not fasten off at end of row 14. Do not turn.

Edging
Working over end sps of each of last 14 rows, tr over end sp of last row, sc over end sp of next row, [tr over end sp of next row, sc over end sp of next row] across to last rnd of Crown, sc in each unworked sc across last rnd of Crown, sc over end sp of first row of Brim on opposite side, tr over end sp of next row, [sc over end sp of next row, tr over end sp of next row] across to last row of Brim, sl st in same sp as last tr. Fasten off.

Finishing
Cut a 28-inch length of ribbon. Weave through rnd 11 on Brim of Bonnet.

BOOTIE
Make 2.
Sole
Rnd 1: Beg at back. Ch 18, *dc in 4th ch,* dc in 4th ch from hook, 2 dc in next ch, dc in each of next 12 ch, 5 dc in last ch; working in rem lps across opposite side of foundation ch, dc in each of next 12 lps, 2 dc in next lp, join with sl st in last ch of ch-18. *(35 dc)*
Rnd 2: Ch 3 *(counts as first dc throughout)*, 2 dc in each of next 3 dc, dc in each of next 11 dc, 2 dc in each of next 6 dc, dc in each of next 11 dc, 2 dc in each of next 3 dc, join with sl st in 3rd ch of beg ch-3. *(47 dc)*
Rnd 3: Ch 3, [2 dc in next dc, dc in next dc] 3 times, dc in each of next 11 dc, [2 dc in next dc, dc in next dc] 6 times, dc in each of next 11 dc, [2 dc in next dc, dc in next dc] twice, 2 dc in each of next 2 dc, join with sl st in 3rd ch of beg ch-3. Do not fasten off. *(60 dc)*

Sides
Rnd 4: Ch 4 *(counts as first dc, ch-1)*, sk next dc, [**bpdc** *(see Special Stitches)* in next dc, ch 1, sk next dc] around, join with sl st in 3rd ch of beg ch-4, turn. *(30 ch-1 sps)*
Rnd 5: Ch 1, sc in same st as joining, tr in each ch-1 sp and sc in each dc around, join with sl st in beg sc, turn. *(30 tr)*
Rnd 6: Ch 4, [dc in next sc, ch 1] around, join with sl st in 3rd ch of beg ch-4, turn. *(30 ch-1 sps)*
Rnds 7 & 8: Rep rnds 5 and 6. Fasten off.

Instep
Row 1: With back of Bootie facing, beg counting with first ch-4 of last rnd of Sides as first dc, count 12 dc to the left; with RS facing, join thread with a sl st in **back lp** *(see Stitch Guide)* only of next dc, ch 4; working in back lp only this row, dc in next dc, [ch 1, dc in next dc] 5 times, turn. *(6 ch-1 sps)*
Row 2: Ch 1, sc in each dc and tr in each ch-1 sp across to first ch-4, tr in ch-4 sp, sc in 3rd ch of ch-4, turn. *(6 tr)*
Row 3: Ch 4, dc in next sc, [ch 1, dc in next sc] across, turn. *(6 ch-1 sps)*

Rows 4 & 5: Rep rows 2 and 3. Fasten off at end of row 5.

Join Instep to Sides
With back of Bootie facing, beg counting with first ch-4 of last rnd of Sides as first dc, count 7 dc to the right; with WS facing, join thread with a sl st in next dc, ch 1, sc in same dc; *working through both thicknesses of Instep and Sides, [tr in next sp on Instep and next sp on Sides at once, sc in end st of next row on Instep and next sp of Sides at once] twice, tr over last sp on Instep and next sp of Sides at once; working in rem lps on last row of Sides at base of Instep, sc in next dc, [tr in next sp, sc in next dc] 6 times, [tr in next end sp on Instep and next sp on Sides at once, sc in end st on next row of Instep and next sp on Sides at once] twice, tr in next sp on Instep and next sp on Sides at once, sc in next dc on Sides. Do not fasten off. Turn. *(14 sps unworked on last rnd of Sides)*

Top
Rnd 1: With RS facing, ch 4, shell in first dc on last row of Instep, ch 1, dc in each of next 2 dc, ch 1, shell in next dc on Instep, ch 1, dc in each of next 2 dc, ch 1, shell in same dc on Sides as joining sc, ch 1, [dc in each of next 2 dc, ch 1, shell in next dc, ch 1] 4 times, dc in next dc, join with sl st in 3rd ch of beg ch-4, turn. *(7 shells)*
Rnd 2: Ch 1; beg in same st as joining, sc in each dc and tr in each ch sp around, join with sl st in beg sc, turn. *(28 tr)*
Rnd 3: Sl st in next tr and next sc, ch 4, *shell in next sc, ch 1, dc in next sc, sk (next tr, next 2 sc, next tr)**, dc in next sc, ch 1, rep from * around, ending last rep at **, join with sl st in 3rd ch of beg ch-4, turn. *(7 shells)*
Rnds 4–6: Rep rnds 2 and 3, then rep rnd 2. At end of rnd 6, fasten off.

Finishing
Cut 2 lengths of ribbon each 15 inches long. Weave 1 length through rnd 8 of Sides and across row 5 of Instep on each Bootie. ❏❏

306 East Parr Road
Berne, IN 46711
© 2005 Annie's Attic

TOLL-FREE ORDER LINE or to request a free catalog (800) LV-ANNIE (800) 582-6643
Customer Service (800) AT-ANNIE (800) 282-6643, **Fax** (800) 882-6643
Visit www.AnniesAttic.com

ISBN: 1-59635-048-2   Printed in USA   3 4 5 6 7 8 9

Stitch Guide

ABBREVIATIONS

beg ....begin/beginning
bpdc ....back post double crochet
bpsc .... back post single crochet
bptr..............back post treble crochet
CC ....contrasting color
ch ....chain stitch
ch- ....refers to chain or space
   previously made (i.e. ch-1 space)
ch sp .... chain space
cl(s) ....cluster(s)
cm ....centimeter(s)
dc ....double crochet
dec..decrease/decreases/decreasing
dtr...................double treble crochet
fpdc ....front post double crochet
fpsc .... front post single crochet
fptr................front post treble crochet
g .... gram(s)
hdc ....half double crochet
inc ......increase/increases/increasing
lp(s)...loop(s)
MC .... main color
mm .... millimeter(s)
oz...ounce(s)
pc .... popcorn
rem .... remain/remaining
rep .... repeat(s)
rnd(s) .... round(s)
RS...right side
sc .... single crochet
sk ....skip/skipped
sl st ....slip stitch
sp(s)...space(s)
st(s)................................... stitch(es)
tog ....together
tr....................................treble crochet
trtr ....triple treble
WS...wrong side
yd(s)..................................yard(s)
yo ....yarn over

Chain—ch: Yo, pull through lp on hook.
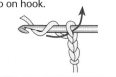

Slip stitch—sl st: Insert hook in st, yo, pull through both lps on hook.

Single crochet—sc: Insert hook in st, yo, pull through st, yo, pull through both lps on hook.
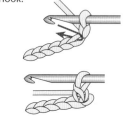

Front loop—front lp
Back loop—back lp
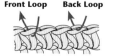

Front post stitch—fp:
Back post stitch—bp: When working post st, insert hook from right to left around post st on previous row.
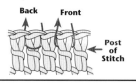

Half double crochet—hdc: Yo, insert hook in st, yo, pull through st, yo, pull through all 3 lps on hook.

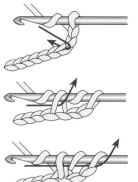

Double crochet—dc: Yo, insert hook in st, yo, pull through st, [yo, pull through 2 lps] twice.
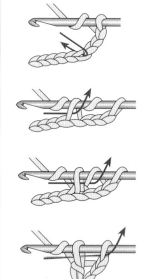

Change colors: Drop first color; with 2nd color, pull through last 2 lps of st.
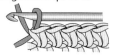

Treble crochet—tr: Yo twice, insert hook in st, yo, pull through st, [yo, pull through 2 lps] 3 times.
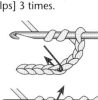

Double treble crochet—dtr: Yo 3 times, insert hook in st, yo, pull through st, [yo, pull through 2 lps] 4 times.

Single crochet decrease (sc dec): (Insert hook, yo, draw up a lp) in each of the sts indicated, yo, draw through all lps on hook.
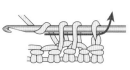
Example of 2-sc dec

Half double crochet decrease (hdc dec): (Yo, insert hook, yo, draw lp through) in each of the sts indicated, yo, draw through all lps on hook.

Example of 2-hdc dec

Double crochet decrease (dc dec): (Yo, insert hook, yo, draw lp through, yo, draw through 2 lps on hook) in each of the sts indicated, yo, draw through all lps on hook.

Example of 2-dc dec

US		UK
sl st (slip stitch)	=	sc (single crochet)
sc (single crochet)	=	dc (double crochet)
hdc (half double crochet)	=	htr (half treble crochet)
dc (double crochet)	=	tr (treble crochet)
tr (treble crochet)	=	dtr (double treble crochet)
dtr (double treble crochet)	=	ttr (triple treble crochet)
skip	=	miss

For more complete information, visit

StitchGuide.com